```
I0111306
```

All Scripture references taken from the KJV of the
Holy Bible, unless otherwise indicated.

~~AUNTIE KAREN~~ ANTI-KAREN: *Mind Your Own Business, Not Other People's*

by Dr. Marlene Miles

Freshwater Press 2026

Freshwaterpress9@gmail.com

ISBN: 978-1-971933-15-3

Paperback Version

Table of Contents

~~AUNTIE KAREN~~ ANTI-KAREN

How to Mind Your Business

Without Minding Other People's

by Dr. Marlene Miles

Freshwater

~~AUNTIE KAREN~~

So many of us have had a sweet auntie growing up. Some of us loved her once. Then we grew up. Maybe her name is really Karen; maybe it's not.

Now she's turned into the person who wants to raise a person that is already raised and she's not even a part of the 'village.' No, village people is a musical group, it is not a card to get you into any place you want and to be in charge there.

Auntie Karen used to be a favorite, maybe the most favorite in a family. She is sweet, attentive and she probably had homemade cookies whether she knew you were coming to visit or not. She gave you a chocolate Easter bunny in the spring and cute toys as gifts for Christmas. You couldn't wait to go to her house because she was your favorite aunt.

This book isn't to bash her; but it is in search of that sweet Auntie Karen. But she has changed from sweet to whatever this is. The posture, the person, the entity or whatever she is, named *Karen* is no longer acceptable, but the person is not erased. Maybe Auntie Karen is still in there and can be redeemed?

She has turned into a Karen, no Auntie title, just Karen. It's not that you two are best friends and she said you can call her by her first name now. Now, she is behaving like a straight up, pure -d, devil of a Karen.

You're not declaring judgment on Auntie Karen, but she has really changed. You're declaring **boundaries against the behavior**.

- *I recognize how this started*
- *I understand how it formed*
- *I refuse to operate this way*
- *But I still believe people can choose differently*

There is a way back — but it requires self-governance. *I saw this in myself, in my family, in my culture — and I chose to stop.*

- **AUNTIE-KAREN** is the posture you choose
- **ANTI KAREN** is the pattern you refuse
- Redemption is possible — but **not without awareness.**

But what do we do with this Auntie Karen who has changed so drastically? Do we hold an intervention?

We defeat it by outgrowing it.

Most Karens didn't wake up wanting to manage strangers. But somehow, they just forgot how to manage themselves and at the same time wanting to manage everyone else.

The good news? This is recoverable.

Relax. This book is for grown people who are just tired.

ANTI-KAREN

I want to be very clear up front: this book is not about hating anyone. It's about minding your business. Which, as it turns out, is a skill. A rare one. A disappearing one. Judging by the current state of public behavior—an endangered one.

At some point in life, many of us knew (or loved) an Auntie Karen. She was helpful. She was concerned. She noticed things. She corrected things. She *meant well.* She also somehow knew what everyone else was doing wrong at all times, including people she had just met in line.

This book is not about canceling Auntie Karen. You'll notice her name is still there—just crossed out. Because this book is about the moment you realize: *Oh. This is not the way.* It's about the day you decide you no longer need to correct strangers, manage environments you don't own, escalate minor inconveniences into character flaws, or supervise adults who did not hire you to mentor, manage, manipulate or maneuver them.

Being anti-Karen is not a vocal protest, nor is it silence. It's self-governance. It's knowing when a thought is just a thought. It's recognizing that discomfort is not an emergency. It's understanding that not everything requires your input, your opinion, your policy knowledge, or your presence.

This is a book for people who have realized that some boundaries don't need announcements. It is for those who have come to know that leaving quietly is often the power move. Now you know that Peace improves dramatically when you stop monitoring other people's choices.

If you've ever thought, *"Why am I even involved in this?"* Congratulations. You're ready.

If you've ever noticed yourself about to say, *"Someone needs to do something,"* and then thought better of it, this book is for you.

And if you're reading this wondering whether you might be a little bit *Karen* sometimes? Relax. Awareness is the exit.

So, I guess I'd better check myself while I'm at it.

WHAT IS MY BUSINESS (AND WHAT IS NOT)

MY BUSINESS ✔

- My body, my time, my money
- My reactions (especially the unspoken ones)
- Whether I stay, leave, or disengage
- What I tolerate repeatedly
- My tone, my volume, my follow-through
- Whether I need to be involved at all
- When something no longer works *for me*

NOT MY BUSINESS ✖

- How grown adults run their lives
- Decisions that don't involve me, affect me, or require my consent
- Teaching lessons no one asked to learn
- Correcting strangers for sport
- Policing preferences, personalities, or vibes
- Enforcing rules I didn't create and can't enforce

- Other people's consequences (especially the ones they insist on earning)

A good rule of thumb: If you're not responsible for fixing it, funding it, or living with it, then it's probably not your business.

JUST BECAUSE YOU NOTICED DOESN'T MEAN YOU'RE ASSIGNED

1. The Line Monitor

She does not work here. She knows who arrived when, who is "cheating," and why the system is flawed. No one asked. This could have been an exit.

2. The Policy Translator

She doesn't work here either, but she *knows the rules*. Or at least her version of them. She begins with, "Actually…" Policies are not a personality.

3. The Volume Coach

She is concerned about how loudly other people are existing. Children. Teenagers. Joy. Laughter. Discomfort is not an emergency.

4. The Concerned Observer

She is "just worried" about choices that do not affect her, involve her, or require her input. She insists it's love. Surveillance is not concern with better lighting.

5. The Escalator

She skipped conversation and went straight to management. She enjoys the walk. This meeting could have been an exit.

6. The Parking Lot Debrief.

The event is over. Everyone else has moved on. She is still talking about it. Some situations end. Others are re-performed.

Noticing is passive. Assignment is active. Confusing the two is how many people end up exhausted, irritated, and oddly proud of themselves for no reason.

You noticed the line was slow, for example. You noticed someone parked crooked. You noticed the music was loud. You noticed a rule wasn't being followed to the letter. Great. Gold star. Observation complete.

None of that means you've been deputized. There is a quiet lie floating around that says, *If I notice it, I'm responsible for it.* That lie turns people into unpaid supervisors of spaces they don't own, fund, or control.

Anti-Karen energy knows this: Awareness is not a summons. Sometimes the most mature response to noticing something is doing absolutely nothing — or better yet, leaving. If you're constantly tired after "handling things," it may be because you're handling what was never handed to you.

THE QUIZ

AM I *KAREN-ING*... OR AM I CAREENING?

(Be honest. No one is grading this.)

Answer **YES** or **NO**:

1. Did I feel compelled to correct someone I will never see again?

2. Did I assume responsibility without being asked?

3. Did I escalate instead of exiting?

4. Did I say "someone needs to do something" and mean *me*?

5. Did I mistake irritation for injustice?

6. Did I quote a rule instead of considering relevance?

7. Did I feel offended on behalf of people who didn't ask me to?

8. Did I stay longer than necessary just to make a point?

9. Did I rehearse a speech that no one requested?

10. Did I feel powerful for about 30 seconds and tired immediately after?

Scoring:

- **0–2 YES:** Congratulations. You are governing yourself.

- **3–5 YES:** You may be circling the parking lot. Exit available.

- **6+ YES:** Step away from the counter. Hydrate. Rejoin society later.

(No shame. Awareness is the off-ramp.)

Anti-Karen isn't about being nicer. It's about being **free**. Freedom improves dramatically when you stop minding other people's business.

DISCOMFORT IS NOT AN EMERGENCY

Somewhere along the way, discomfort got promoted to crisis. This is not about danger, harm, or injustice. It's just... *I don't like this.* Suddenly, someone must intervene, someone must explain. Someone must adjust. Someone must be informed.

Discomfort feels urgent because we are humans and we don't tolerate discomfort very well. Discomfort wants relief. But urgency does not automatically equal responsibility.

You can be uncomfortable and still be safe. You can be annoyed and still be fine. You can dislike something and still keep moving. Anti-Karen energy understands a very mature truth: **Not every feeling requires action.**

Sometimes the appropriate response to discomfort is waiting, adjusting internally, leaving, or doing absolutely nothing.

This applies even when the music is loud. Even when the rules are bent. It is applies when the vibes are *off*, or someone else is enjoying themselves incorrectly.

Discomfort does not appoint you as hall monitor. If you feel the urge to correct, pause and ask, *Is this harmful — or merely irritating?* If the answer is "irritating," congratulations. You have just identified a growth opportunity.

Growth looks like silence, tolerance, and occasionally, an exit. Not a speech.

POLICIES ARE NOT A LOVE LANGUAGE

Some people express care with words. Some with acts of service. Some with gifts. Karen expresses care with **policies**. She doesn't say: "How can I help?" She's not there as a helper or a good Samaritan. She's there for herself, not for you. She says, "That's not how it's done." Whatever she says, the unspoken part is, *This is offending **me***.

She doesn't ask, "What do you need?" She announces, "There's a rule about that."

Policies are useful. They are necessary. They are not affectionate. Quoting a policy does not make you helpful, righteous, correct, or friendly. It makes you **informational**. Information without invitation is just noise. A download of rules and regulations could make the speaker confrontational, and put the hearer on defense.

Anti-Karen energy knows that rules exist to serve people, not that people exist to serve rules. If you didn't create the policy, don't enforce the policy, and won't suffer the consequences of the policy being broken— you may simply... let it go.

Wild, I know.

A good test: *Am I enforcing this rule because it matters — or because it makes me feel important?* If it's the second one, congratulations again. You've discovered another exit.

I'm anti-Karen.

I'm not internet-culture loud, but clarifying. Karen" isn't a person. It's a mode of operating.

Anti-Karen is not silence or passivity. It's refusing to outsource your authority to public confrontation.

People who govern themselves don't need to govern others. Karen Energy is relying on external control, and public escalation. Karen energy demands compliance, and moral performance. Karen says, "Someone must fix this." Authority is borrowed from outrage.

Anti-Karen energy, on the other hand, employs internal self-governance, private decision-making, clean and clear exits. Anti-Karen does not require an audience. Anti-Karen is moving in their own authority.

Anti-Karen does not react to *Karen* culture. Anti-Karen has never been in it, and she doesn't accuse, campaign, confront, or demand explanations. Anti-Karen does not try to manage others' behavior; she only observes, decides, and makes her move.

Anti-Karen is often quiet, but that is not a sign of weakness. It may take more strength to remain quiet than it takes to be loud and boisterous in many situations.

Anti-Karens are more likely to say things like, "Nothing illegal was happening. I simply decided I would not be participating further." "I didn't need to speak to a manager. I needed to leave." "Some people escalate. I update my calendar." "I'm not mad. I'm unavailable."

She may further say, "I did not ask to speak to anyone. I didn't need customer service. I needed distance."

Anti-Karen is very wise.

THE *spirit* of KAREN

The *spirit of Karen* is not female; it has no gender. It is the *spirit* of externalized control. It manifests as: Policing instead of governing. It is escalation instead of exit. It is correction instead of discernment. It is outrage instead of boundaries.

Who is Karen most like in the Bible? (Spoiler: It's not who people usually think.) We will start with **Miriam who has a style of public moral policing**. Miriam didn't rebel in secret. She spoke publicly, cloaking complaint in righteousness. "Has the Lord spoken only through Moses?" Translation: "Who put you in charge?" "I deserve a say." "This isn't fair." Karen energy here feels entitled to a megaphone or a microphone. The Karen *spirit* frames grievance as justice. It confuses proximity with authority.

Miriam didn't need discernment. She needed her lane back.

Jezebel represents institutional control, not the seductive version. This is the administrative Jezebel, not the caricature. She weaponizes rules. She uses letters, systems, and authority. She outsources cruelty to process. She never looks like the villain. This is real Karen energy. She might say something like, "I'll escalate this." "I know the policy." "Someone needs to be held accountable."

Jezebel chases Elijah. The prophet of God was right; the prophets of Baal were wrong. Jezebel declares herself right and harasses or pursues those who she has deemed as wrong.

Diotrephes represents control through gatekeeping. Found in 3 John 9-11, he is a local pastor who refused to receive those sent by God, specifically the Apostle John. The Bible literally says Diotrephes loved to be first. Rejected others Blocked access. Talked excessively. All that is Karen energy; she likes to control the room and decide who *belongs*. She confuses management with leadership.

Eliab was offended by someone else's assignment. Eliab wasn't wrong about David's youth, he was wrong about his own authority. Karen energy: "Why are you here?" "Who sent you?" "This isn't appropriate."

"If I'm uncomfortable, someone else must change." That is false.

The Truth is: "If I'm uncomfortable, I must decide." This is what Anti-Karen knows through Wisdom.

TIME OF LIFE

Karen is not a menopause or perimenopause diagnosis. So don't try it. Hormonal transition can lower tolerance and amplify reactions, which *can* make ungoverned patterns more visible if they already exist.

Perimenopause and menopause can involve real, documented changes such as heightened irritability, sensory sensitivity to noise, heat, or clutter. There can be sleep disruption which leads to a lower emotional buffer. There can be anxiety spikes, reduced stress tolerance and feeling overwhelmed by stimuli that never used to bother you at all. It can show up as decreased patience for ambiguity or disorder. Yes, *"everything bothers me"* is a known, temporary physiological reality for many people when it comes to menopause or perimenopause. There are nearly 200 different symptoms of menopause and perimenopause, thankfully no one has all 200 of them.

That's chemistry.

Menopause does not create entitlement, false authority, public policing behavior, escalation addiction, ownership of other people's choices, obsession with control, need for an audience, or misuse of systems or rules. Those are governance issues, not hormone issues.

Hormones can reduce coping capacity; they do not install a Pharisee operating system. Hormonal transition amplifies what's already there. It does not invent new moral frameworks. So, a self-governing person in menopause may become quieter, not louder. More selective, more boundary-conscious, more withdrawn, and more protective of peace.

A control-oriented person in menopause may become more reactive, more easily offended, more externalizing, more intrusive, more escalatory. Same stressor; different operating system.

Karen may appear more often in this *season* but realize that menopause is not the creator of Karens. And remember the spirit of Karen travels in males and females.

Yet, in peri- and menopause there is a reduced tolerance for ambiguity and foolishness. When internal equilibrium is shaky, external control feels stabilizing. Some people self-soothe by resting, simplifying, withdrawing, or asking for help. Others self-soothe by correcting, organizing people, enforcing rules, or demanding order *outside* themselves. That second response is where Karen-energy shows up.

During this season in a woman's life there may be loss of old identity structures. Midlife transitions can unsettle roles, relevance, visibility, influence, desirability. Some people respond with introspection, reinvention, or humility. Others respond with territoriality, moral superiority, rule enforcement, and the "someone must be in charge" attitude.

Again, not hormones. It's more of a response to loss of control. Hormones can shorten patience, but they don't create entitlement. Menopause may make everything louder, but it doesn't decide where authority belongs.

KAREN-TOSTERONE

Men have midlife hormonal shifts (yes, andropause is real). Symptoms of andropause my show up as irritability, rigidity, territorial behavior, policing tendencies. They just do it **with different costumes**. They can look like the HOA president, the church elder, the parking-lot enforcer, comment-section referee, workplace gatekeeper.

Same *spirit*. Different packaging.

Karen-tosterone is not a hormone, it's a word I made up to make a point. It's the sudden surge of confidence that convinces a person they have authority they were never given: assumed authority. It produces symptoms such as rule-quoting, escalation, territorial behavior, and an urgent need to "do something" — usually involving other people's lives.

"Karen-tosterone" (is behavioral *energy*, not biology. Karen often flows in male, institutional authority patterns. It's not about women acting like men. It's not about men acting like women. It's not saying that hormones make you bad. It is borrowed dominance without assignment.

Karen-tosterone explains the proud, chest-out posture. It explains the *"We can't let them get away with this" energy*. It explains the need to dominate space, and the confidence-to-competence gap. Both men and women have the real hormone testosterone, so this 'karen-tosterone' is that impetus that makes a person step up, step out and do something bold, although that bold thing ma not be expedient or even right.

Karenisol (noun) is the fake phantom hormone of false authority. It is a fictional stress compound released during minor inconvenience, producing heightened vigilance, territorial behavior, and an urgent desire to intervene. It is male-female, gender balanced, equal opportunity.

Symptoms may include rule-quoting, escalation impulses, clipboard confidence, moral certainty without assignment, and a deep intolerance for quiet exits or being ignored.

Triggers include, but are not limited to: trash cans, restaurant seating, bylaws, comment sections. and other people minding their business. **Side effects are** temporary sense of authority, chronic dissatisfaction, all leading to exhaustion in surrounding humans.

Important note *Karenisol is not a hormone. It's a response to discomfort combined with false jurisdiction.*

- Karenisol spikes when no one asked for help.

- High Karenisol environments around normal and Anti-Karens require clean exits.

- "Lower your Karenisol. Raise your boundaries."

- "Karenisol thrives where roles are unclear."

Karen-tosterone creates confidence without credentials, making people boldly go where they probably shouldn't be going. Again, it is the fake, mysterious, invisible hormone that makes people Karen-like and it affects men too. They just call it *being thorough.*

Menopause can make stimuli harder to tolerate. Karen behavior is about where discomfort gets discharged. If the expression is inward, that is self-governance. If it is expressed outwardly those are attempts at control.

KARENISOL RECEPTORS

Some people get intoxicated on false power, and others do not. *Why is that?* It's because not everyone exposed to the fake, just coined word, Karenisol become *Karens*. Even Auntie Karen, who used to be sweet, starts to behave weirdly if she has Karenisol receptors in her system. Those who get a release of this Karenisol into their system all react the same way. Some people feel it surge... and then it passes and they do not act on it.

Others absorb it, amplify it, and begin supervising strangers. The difference isn't temperament, it's whose got the Karenisol receptors. It's about who is likely to become a Karen.

Karenisol receptors tend to develop in people who learned early that order = safety. Or that control = worth. Vigilance = responsibility, or if they remain silent that equals danger.

Common traits are high anxiety; they can stay activated a long time. Another trait is their identity is tied to being "the responsible one." They have discomfort with ambiguity, and they fear that things may be "slipping." They also believe that inaction equals failure.

These people don't just feel Karenisol, they **bind** to it. Once bound, Karenisol produces confidence without assignment, urgency without proportion, authority without consent. That's when behavior shifts from awareness to enforcement.

Some people are naturally Karenisol-resistant. They experience the same triggers: the trash can, the rule violation, the awkward moment, the imperfection. But instead of escalating, they think, "Huh. Interesting." And move on.

These people tend to have strong internal boundaries, comfort with disorder, confidence in self-governance, low need for external validation, lived experience with choosing Peace.

Healthy boundaries say, "That's not mine to manage, but I still care about people." Indifference says, "That's not my business, and I don't care what happens." The first comes from Peace; the other comes from disengagement. One is calm; The other is cold. One knows when to step back; the other never steps forward.

Anti-Karen is not apathetic; she minds her business without losing her humanity.

Karenisol enters… and then **exits if there is nothing in a person to link them with this fake hormone, then there is no** binding. No drama. Karenisol doesn't activate power. It activates **permission hunger**.

People with Karenisol *receptors* are not addicted to control, they are addicted to **relief**. There is something in them that connects with the drama, so they act out. Control gives temporary relief from the anxiety of whatever is driving them to want to 'do something about something or someone who is "wrong." This is not for the good of mankind necessarily--, this is personal; it's for Karen, herself.

That's why escalation feels calming. Doing something feels righteous. Enforcement feels stabilizing. Until it doesn't.

Anti-Karen people slough it off. Anti-Karen types have already learned not every discomfort is actionable. Not every problem is theirs. Not every rule violation is personal. Not every silence is dangerous. They don't need relief through control.

They already have Peace.

Karenisol only binds where Peace is outsourced. If you govern yourself, Karenisol has nowhere to land. Karenisol needs receptors. Boundaries block them. Some people metabolize stress. Others weaponize it.

Karenisol binds easily here because **Law without Grace requires enforcement**. Common phrases include *That's not the point. Rules are rules. If we let this slide…* Or, *Someone has to uphold standards.* Karenisol thrives where obedience matters more than outcomes, correctness matters more than people, and where enforcement replaces Wisdom.

Who also hath made us able ministers of the new testament; not of the letter, but of the spirit: for the letter killeth, but the spirit giveth life. (2 Corinthians 3:6)

Grace-governed people understand that rules exist to serve life. Mercy is not disorder. Context matters. Wisdom outranks enforcement. They can see the same infraction and think "I'm not called to that." Or, "That's not worth my Peace."

Grace-governed people don't panic at imperfection. They don't moralize inconvenience. They don't need to correct everything they notice. They don't feel responsible for outcomes they weren't assigned.

"…but the Spirit gives life."

Karenisol hates Grace. Grace removes leverage, dissolves outrage, neutralizes authority theater. Grace says, "I could act… but I won't." Grace walks away.

Karenisol cannot survive that thought process.

When faced with disorder, ask: *Do I feel compelled to enforce — or free to discern? If you feel* compelled, then Karenisol is ruling you. If you feel free then you live in Karenoshen. (a made up place for the purposes of this book, akin to *Goshen*, where God's people live.)

Goshen was where God's people lived. They were protected while chaos happened elsewhere, spared from plagues affecting Egypt. Governed by Grace and covering. Amen. *There is a place you can live where Karenisol doesn't touch you. That place is named Karenoshen.*

- **Karenisol** → the stress compound (Law, control, enforcement)

- **Karenoshen** → the protected operating zone (Grace, discernment, Peace)

Karenoshen is the Grace-governed place where Karenisol has no jurisdiction. It is a mindset, a posture, and a way of living where unnecessary enforcement cannot enter.

Karenoshen is where you live when you stop patrolling Egypt.

Karenisol rages in Egypt, in the unsaved and the un-converted, but it cannot enter Karenoshen. Anti-Karen lives there and she says:

- "I don't fight Karen energy. I live in Karenoshen."

- "Karenoshen is quiet. That's how you know you're safe."

- "You don't need to confront Pharaoh if you live in Goshen." There is no Karen in Karenoshen.

- "Karenoshen requires no hall monitors."

Choosing to live a certain way --, the way of foolishness. Instead, you can say, "I live somewhere else." And that's very God-like; that's very Jesus.

Karen will remain Karen; she is not imbued with Grace.

TV KARENS – OLD SCHOOL

Karen may think she's new; she's not. There is nothing new under the sun, including Ms. Karen. The TV show, **Bewitched** featured a nosy next door neighbor, Mrs. Kravitz. She is an early, textbook Karen prototype. The writers absolutely knew what they were doing.

Mrs. Kravitz was a "Karen" and with a twist. Mrs. Gladys Kravitz (*Bewitched*, 1960s) embodies proto-Karen energy before the term existed. She is what Karen looks like before escalation culture had managers and hotlines.

Mrs. Kravitz's Karen credentials; she checks nearly every box:

1. **Hyper-Surveillance** - Watches neighbors constantly, Notices everything, Interprets neutrality as suspicious. Classic Karen: *If I see it, I must report it.*

2. **Territorial Fixation** - Feels ownership over the neighborhood. Treats public space like private jurisdiction. Gladys Kravitz is the neighborhood watch of the suburbs.

3. **Escalation Addiction**. Mrs. Kravitz runs to authority figures (husband, police, doctors) and can't let go of anything. She needs validation that she's *right*. *But when* authority dismisses her, that doesn't stop her; she escalates again.

4. **Moral Certainty Without Proof**. Ironic, Mrs. Kravitz is usually right; Samantha *is* a whole witch. Weird things *are* happening. But Gladys Kravitz has no assignment, no authority and no proof that anyone will accept. She is the perfect Karen metaphor.

Mrs. Kravitz isn't malicious, but she is unassigned and obsessed. Her tragedy isn't evil — it's fixation, lack of self-governance and she is unable to let it go, to disengage. She cannot stop monitoring. The more she escalates, the less credible she becomes.

Mrs. Kravitz believes that if she can see it, then it's her business.

Anti-Karen believes, "If it's not my life, it's not my business."

Mrs. Kravitz watches from the curtain. Anti-Karen closes the curtain and makes tea. Same neighborhood. Different people; very different posture.

That's Karen's curse in a nutcase. I mean nutshell.

CAM WINSTON

The Frasier Condo Association President = Male Karen

Cam Winston. He wasn't emotional. He wasn't loud. He wasn't hysterical. Which is exactly why he's dangerous-adjacent and hilarious. What made him Karen-coded

1. **Authority Without Relationship** He didn't *know* people; he regulated them. Everything was policy-first, humanity second. That's Karen energy in a designer tweed jacket with suede patches on the elbows.

2. **Rule Worship Obsessed** with bylaws, procedures, approvals. He used documents as weapons. He confused governance with control. The classic Karen trait, *"I'm not being difficult — I'm enforcing the rules."*

Sir. Sit down.

He displays territorial fixation. To him, the building wasn't a community; it was his jurisdiction.

He took personal offense at noncompliance. He acted as if residents were guests in *his* space. Karen doesn't ask, *"Does this matter?"* Karen asks, *"Why wasn't I consulted?"*

He had a system that he worked; he escalated through process. Unlike the female Karen who goes straight to the manager, Male Karen **becomes** the manager. Same *spirit*; better infrastructure. The Karen *spirit* often flows in male institutional *spirits*.

Frasier himself is neurotic but self-aware. The condo president is unaware and empowered. His seriousness makes him absurd. We laugh because control without joy always looks ridiculous.

- Female Karen → escalates to authority

- Male Karen → *becomes* authority

Same posture in both: entitlement, surveillance, enforcement, obsession with order. Same posture: different outfit.

Some Karens ask to speak to the manager. Others run for the board. Karen isn't gendered but Karen is credentialed.

Yes — the Frasier condo president is a Karen. HOA Karen, Clipboard Karen, Bylaw Karen, Institutional Karen.

Karen is not about personality. Karen is about misplaced authority. And that would be Cam Winston. Cam Winston — the smug, impeccably dressed, ultra-competent condo board president, played by Brian Stokes Mitchell, instantly became Frasier's archnemesis in the building. He lived upstairs, had better amenities, better parties, better everything. Frazier was so jealous. But still, Cam is peak Male Institutional Karen. He is polished, credentialed, calm. quietly territorial and fully weaponized with competence.

All this is exactly why Frasier *hated* him.

Cam already owns the system. Some Karens ask for the manager. Cam Winston already **is** the manager. Frazier deeply coveted that position. Which is why Frasier lost his mind. You can't out-escalate someone who's already escalated. He is already institutionalized. Cam doesn't patrol the mall; he *owns the mall*.

BARNEY FIFE

Mayberry, USA.

Barney Fife was 100% Karen. Barney Fife without the uniform, without the badge is absolutely a Karen. Barney Fife is the Proto-Karen — the blueprint before the name existed.

The uniform gives Barney *just enough* legitimacy, masks insecurity as authority, and turns anxiety into enforcement.

Without the uniform, you're left with hyper-vigilance, rule obsession, for others. But rule obsession is usually only for others. Without the uniform there is only performance of authority, a deep fear of disorder, and the constant need to be seen as important. That's Karen energy in sepia tone, because the Andy Grffith show was filmed back in the day, was in black and white.

Barney Fife Karen Traits (Checklist)

☑ Over-identifies with authority
☑ Quotes rules constantly

☑ Escalates small issues

☑ Patrols space compulsively

☑ Needs validation from superiors

☑ Takes himself very seriously

☑ Lacks proportional response

☑ Panics when ignored

☑ Is more invested in *order* than *outcomes*

Classic.

Barney is *funny* (and Karen often isn't). Barney is insecure, not entitled. He *wants* to be useful, and he doesn't outsource punishment for sport. This is why we laugh *with* Barney.

Karen, by contrast offloads consequence, hides behind systems, insists on escalation, and refuses self-reflection. Barney *could* be redeemed. Karen resists redemption because she thinks she's already right.

Barney Fife without a uniform is just a Karen with a whistle. Give insecurity a badge and it becomes Barney. Take the badge away and it becomes Karen. Barney Fife without his sheriff's uniform is Karen, Mayberry Edition. *Barney is an example of authority gone sideways*.

Typical Barney: "Andy, we've got to do something about that. We can't let them get away with that, can we Andy? Andy?" Barney was a real forerunner. He was Karen-**before-Karen**.

The following is Barney speak, translated into Anti-Karen theology:

- *"Something must be done"* → false urgency

- *"We can't let them"* → imagined jurisdiction

- *"Get away with"* → moralized irritation

- *"Andy?"* → appeal to higher authority for validation

Barney: "Andy, we've got to do something about that."

Anti-Karen reply (Andy): "No, Barney. We actually don't."

"Karen's favorite sentence always ends the same way: *'...can we?'*" That's the tell: If you were assigned, you wouldn't need permission. If it mattered, it wouldn't require escalation. If it were your business, you wouldn't be pleading for backup.

Barney isn't evil. He's anxious, ungoverned, and desperate to *matter*.

KAREN-ADJACENT

Paul Blart, Mall Cop is Karen-adjacent, but with a crucial difference that actually makes him hilarious *and* sympathetic.

Paul Blart is not exactly a Karen, but he is Karen-coded. He *looks* Like a Karen because he checks several external boxes. He is obsessive about rules. He over-identifies with authority; he is somebody. He patrols space intensely and takes himself way too seriously. Paul Blart treats the mall like sacred ground.

Karen alert. But here's where he diverges. Paul Blart Is *Not* a Karen because he actually has an assignment and that matters more than anything. Paul Blart works there—he is literally hired to guard the mall. He has responsibility, and bears real risk. He shows up when it counts. Karen, on the other hand, wants authority without assignment. She has deputized herself. Blart has assignment — and maybe too much enthusiasm. Karen just wants to run this and by this, she wants to control one certain person or one certain group of people who offend her just by their presence.

Blart absorbs cost personally.

Karen escalates and lets others pay the price.

Blart puts himself in danger. Karen brings the danger; she is the cause of it by her ridiculous acts. Blart gets hurt and looks foolish. Karen could get hurt although she really wants that to be the result for others. And, yes, Karen looks foolish, but you'd never get her to believe that.

Blart does show some bravery, courage and accountability. Karen believes she is above the situation that she has seen, weighed, and judged. She is now in the process of the execution of the verdict that she has come up with.

Blart is no Karen. Blart's control is rooted in care, not entitlement.

Blart's motivation isn't superiority, moral or ethnic or cultural policing, or entitlement, but Karen's is all that. Blart's motivation is purpose, dignity, belonging, and wanting to matter. That is a person trying, even if awkwardly trying to be useful.

That's not Karen.

Karen enforces rules to feel important. Blart enforces rules because it's literally his job. Karen wants a badge. Blart *has* a badge — even if it's laminated and sad.

Paul Blart is overzealous, socially awkward, over committed, with misplaced confidence. It is not entitled, escalatory, or territorial without assignment.

He's not Karen. He's mall cop energy done earnestly. Paul Blart isn't a Karen. He's what happens when the mall cop actually cares. "Karen patrols imaginary malls; Blart patrols a real one.

MODERN KAREN PROTOTYPES (BY AGE + PLATFORM)

1. The HOA Facebook Admin (Gen X / Older Millennial). This is the **evolved Karen**. Runs the neighborhood Facebook group, and by runs, I mean, runs it into the ground. Posts every day or every other day when she's busy. "Just a reminder…"

This Karen posts at 6:14 a.m.: "Just a reminder that trash cans must be returned within TWO HOURS of pickup." Comments are turned off. A stock photo of a clipboard is attached.

Knows everyone's trash schedule, dog habits, and parking sins. Locks comments but posts opinions. Uses phrases like:

- o "For visibility"
- o "Per the bylaws"
- o "This affects all of us"

Karen score (out of 5): ⭐ ⭐ ⭐ ⭐ ⭐

This is **institutional authority + surveillance +**

territory. No trash was harmed. Several neighbors were spiritually inconvenienced.

Karen didn't ask to speak to the manager. She became *the* admin.

2. The TikTok 'Call-Out' Woman (Millennial).

She films herself correcting strangers, confronting workers, "educating" people in public. Or, narrating moral superiority in real time. She needs **an audience**.

Karen score: ⭐ ⭐ ⭐ ⭐

This is **public correction + escalation + performance.** *Karen* upgraded from customer service to content creation.

3. The 'HR-Brained' Coworker (All Ages, Corporate)

She's not HR, but *thinks* like HR. She weaponizes policy language. She is "Just documenting this." She CCs people unnecessarily. Frames control as professionalism. She says things like, "I'm just looping in leadership--, for visibility."

No conflict existed until the email. *Some Karens don't escalate verbally. They CC.*

Karen score: ⭐ ⭐ ⭐ ⭐ ⭐

This m**ale or female, totally gender-neutral Karen shows up this way.**

Some Karens don't ask for the manager. They CC them.

She films herself correcting a stranger in public. The caption says: "Hold people accountable."

The comments say: "Yasss queen."

The stranger just wanted coffee. *Karen upgraded from customer service to content creation.*

4. Concerned Church Lady (Gen X / Boomer). She isn't leadership, but acts like oversight. She couches control in prayer language. Some of her phrases may include:

- "I'm just discerning something..."
- "Have you considered..."
- "I felt *led* to say..."

Karen score: ✰ ✰ ✰ ✰ ✰

This is **Pharisee energy with a Bible verse.**

4. The Church 'Concern'

She corners you after service, saying, "I've been praying about you." You didn't ask her anything. You didn't request prayer. You did not apply for oversight. She sighs heavily anyway.

Karen loves Jesus; she just thinks He deputized her.

5. The 'Rules Are Rules' Gym / Airport / School Parent (Millennial).

This one polices behavior that doesn't affect them. They enforce policies selectively. They get angry at flexibility; they are the letter of the law types. They also escalate fast.

Karen score: ⭐⭐⭐⭐

This is **territorial anxiety + rule worship.** Karen isn't protecting order. She's protecting predictability. **The Gym / Airport Enforcer does not** work there. But she knows the rules, the tone, and the "proper way." Flexibility offends her spirit and that's ironic both for a gym and an airport where flexibility is desperately needed. She has promoted herself to chief compliance officer.

Karen isn't protecting order. She's protecting predictability.

6. The Male Karen: Podcast Comment Section Guy (Millennial / Gen Z)

Another modern male Karen is pedantic, and corrective. He has "Actually…" energy and argues definitions instead of substance. He feels responsible for *truth* online. He is among the 'truth' police and a lot of them have their own channels for real.

Karen score: ⭐⭐⭐⭐

This is also **Pharisee spirit; no territory needed.** Karen isn't always loud, sometimes he's quietly but noticeably in the comments.

7. The 'Mom Influencer' Policing Choices (Millennial). This one judges other parents publicly. Frames preferences as moral superiority.

- "Real moms don't…"

- "If you cared about your kids…"

Karen score: ☆ ☆ ☆ ☆

Here, you're looking at **relational control + moral framing.** Karen doesn't want to raise her kids. She wants to supervise yours. She has anointed herself leader of the village that it is going to take to raise those kids -- other people's kids, that is. Hers are fine; there is nothing wrong with her kids because they are perfect because they are hers, or because she already raised them perfectly.

Karen evolves with technology, but her operating system stays the same. Every generation has Karens. They just get new platforms.

FIND YOUR KAREN

Field Guide

1. Did someone notice a problem?

☐ Yes   ☐ No

If no, congratulations — this is not a Karen situation.

2. Does the problem directly affect them?

☐ Yes → Proceed cautiously (could be legitimate)
☐ No → ⚠ Potential Karen activity detected

3. Did they intervene anyway?

☐ Yes   ☐ No

If yes, continue.

4. Did they quote a rule, policy, or "how things are supposed to be"?

☐ Yes   ☐ No

If yes, Karenisol levels may be rising.

5. Did they escalate? (Check all that apply)

☐ Asked to speak to someone
☐ Filed a complaint
☐ CC'd leadership
☐ Posted publicly
☐ "Just wanted to document this"
☐ Involved authorities / management / the internet

Two or more checked = confirmed Karen escalation.

6. Did they resist a quiet exit?

☐ Became offended when ignored
☐ Felt disrespected by silence
☐ Demanded acknowledgment
☐ Interpreted disengagement as rebellion

If yes, you are no longer guessing.

FINAL CONFIRMATION QUESTION

Did they believe the situation required supervision simply because they noticed it?

☐ Yes → CLASSIC KAREN
☐ No → Possibly just annoyed. Grace may still apply.

BONUS INDICATORS (Not diagnostic, but telling)

☐ Strong feelings about trash cans
☐ Clipboard energy
☐ Tight smile
☐ "This affects everyone"
☐ "We can't let this slide"
☐ Treats public space like inherited property

ANTI-KAREN RESPONSE (MEMORIZE THIS)

Not everything you notice is yours to manage.

Or, if you're already in Karenoshen:

Okay.
(exit quietly)

Footnote (Important):

Not every complaint is Karen.
Not every boundary is control.
But authority without assignment always leaves a trail.

THE BIBLICAL KARENS

You don't even have to stretch Scripture to find Karen. There are Biblical male figures who behave Karen-esque. She is most like the Pharisees (Collective). Jesus' sharpest rebukes were aimed at the Pharisees, yet they were supposed to not be sinners. "You bind heavy burdens, grievous to be borne, and lay them on men's shoulders…"

Karen energy: Burden binding, zero-burden-carrying, maximum commentary: these are Pharisees.

Saul is control without assignment. Saul policed outcomes. Justified himself publicly. Blamed others. Couldn't release authority. Karen energy echoes this: *"This shouldn't be happening." "Someone must fix this." "This isn't how it's done."*

Karen operates in a Pharisaical stream — and that stream is male-coded in Scripture. Karen as a Pharisee pattern (not a personality, not a woman) In the Bible, the Pharisees are not primarily immoral. They are over-moral in the wrong way. Their core traits: External righteousness. Public correction. Rule enforcement without relational authority. Love of visibility. Escalation through systems. Control disguised as holiness. Karen is flowing in or impersonating male spirits. Karen adopts an authority posture that was Biblically masculine, institutional, and hierarchical, all without assignment.

Karen is more Pharisaical, than Jezebellish. People often mislabel Karen as Jezebel. Karen does not seduce or manipulate through intimacy.

Jezebel is administrative; she weaponized letters. Pharaoh weaponized oversight. Karen does both, without really knowing why. Jezebel uses manipulation for agenda. Pharaoh uses control for safety. Karen is trying to feel safe and that makes her Pharaonic at the core.

She does not operate relationally. Karen quotes rules. She cites and appeals to policy, even if the rules are made up or self-interpreted. Even if these rules are from another century whose time has passed, if they are convenient for her to use, that's what she will use.

Karen is not a time traveler; she is stuck. Time is moving on; she most often is not.

Karen polices behavior. She corrects publicly; she demands escalation. She uses institutions as weapons, and that's more Pharisee than Jezebel.

Karen is not just seen in women. She is not just a personality; she is an entire Operating System.

1. **The Pharisees — Righteous Without Assignment.** They: corrected publicly, enforced rules they didn't carry, escalated constantly, and confused holiness with supervision. They were right about the law. They were wrong about authority.

Karen trait: "If I see it, I must fix it."

Jesus' response was rarely debate. He divinely fixed what He was sent to fix, because He was Jesus. There is no indication that Jesus ever 'fixed" anything in His flesh. His acts were Divine and miraculous, right? Jesus did not operate as a handyman of circumstances. He operated as the Source of Life, and the changes people saw were the overflow of that.

He didn't "fix" things the way we think of fixing (tuning, adjusting, managing). He didn't repair; He restored. He healed, commanded, forgave, raised, fed, calmed. His acts presented as Divine Authority, not technical repair. He didn't "repair." He restored, and that is spiritual work.

Even though His dad was a carpenter, Jesus' works are never presented as skilled human intervention. They are presented as divine authority over creation, disease, nature, sin, and death.

Even when He touches (eyes, ears, mud on eyes), the text never frames it as technique. Its authority expressed through action.

Jesus did not come to fix broken things. He came to restore what only God can restore.

So, if Karen is not moving divinely, miraculously, and perhaps she is, since Jesus commanded the storm to be still, so Karen tries to command. Jesus moved in Divine authority; Karen is flowing in human overreach. Jesus moved from identity, alignment, and authority. While Karen moves from anxiety, discomfort, and the need to control.

Oh Karen: When you're unsettled inside, the kindest thing you can do for everyone is pause, not manage. Love, Anti-Karen.

When someone isn't grounded, clear, or settled inside, attempts to "take charge" usually create more turbulence than order. So, the wiser move isn't control. It's pause. Distance. Reset. Even a parent knows not to dole out punishment on their own child when they are upset with their kid.

When someone slips into watchman/overseer mode, they start scanning for problems everywhere. And sometimes they *are* noticing something off. The frustration comes from this gap. *I can see it* but *I don't actually have the role, authority, or means to address it. But I'll just go over there and try something anyway. After all, I'm Karen.*

The tension is this: Not every problem is yours to solve. Mind your own business, not other people's. Not every issue is within your jurisdiction; this really is none of your business. Not every disturbance can be handled by management or correction.

A calmer, healthier posture is, "I see it. I don't own it. I will not strain myself trying to control it." *This isn't mine to fix. I don't have jurisdiction here. This isn't my role.* They can't reach it in the moment.

Emotion is louder than insight. That's why the behavior looks so irrational from the outside. It's not a lack of knowledge. It's that the knowledge is temporarily eclipsed by the emotional surge.

In scary situations, the brain can flip into threat-response mode (fight/flight/freeze). When that happens thinking narrows, curiosity and urgency spike. good judgment drops. The need to *do something* overrides the instinct to step back. So instead of "This is dangerous, therefore, leave." You get: "Something is wrong. I have to go see."

Because from the outside, with a regulated nervous system, the right choice is obvious. That's the difference between calm observer vs. activated Karen. Man, she just walked up on us, yelling…is what a person may say of a Karen.

2. Eliab — Offended Gatekeeper. Eliab wasn't wicked, he was offended by someone else's assignment. Karen energy: "Why are you here?" "Who do you think you are?" "This is inappropriate."

Karen is female embodiment of a male institutional *spirit*. She is in unsanctioned authority-mode. No one assigned her to anything. She is attempting correction without relationship; she into the village assigned to raise a child and the person she's talking to (yelling at) is a whole adult. Visibility without responsibility; she can see it, but it has nothing to do with her. That's why Karen often sounds official, quotes policy, invokes "rules" and demands escalation.

She is impersonating authority, not expressing femininity. "I'm not dealing with a personality problem — I'm dealing with a Pharisaical operating system." And once you see that, the response is obvious: You don't argue with Pharisees. You disengage and walk on. Which is exactly what you do. Karen is not a woman problem. Karen is a Pharisee in a wig.

. The proper counter-spirit (Biblically) Jesus didn't confront Pharisees by: escalating, arguing, policy, or defending Himself endlessly. No, He refused traps, answered briefly, and or walked away. Jesus governed Himself and that's Anti-Karen behavior on 100; and it's Christlike.

Karen can operate under the Pharoah or Laban *spirits* too. This "Karen" isn't always just one *spirit*; it's a behavioral convergence that can draw from several ownership-based operating systems already named in Scripture.

"If I am present, **I own.**"

Not: "I steward" "I'm assigned" "I'm responsible" But: "This belongs to me." "I have a say here." "I can intervene." This is why it often operates unconsciously — including in people who are otherwise loving, moral, or religious.

David's older brother. Eliab wasn't wicked. He was triggered by someone else's calling. "Why have you come down here?" "With whom have you left those few sheep?" Translation: *Who do you think you are? You don't belong here. This isn't your place.* Karen is known *for p*olicing access to spaces she doesn't own—and she's not even the police, so there's that, too. She behaves as if she has universal jurisdiction and she does not. Eliab was right about David's youth, but wrong about David's assignment.

3. **Saul displays control masquerading as responsibility.** Saul couldn't release control without panic. He justified himself publicly and blamed others. escalated when insecure punished independence. Saul didn't want obedience. He wanted reassurance.

"This shouldn't be happening." Karen energy panics when people move freely.

4. **Miriam — Public Moral Policing**. Miriam didn't rebel privately. She spoke publicly, cloaking grievance in righteousness: "Has the Lord spoken only through Moses?" Broadcasting concern as virtue. Miriam didn't need clarity. She needed her lane back.

5. **Diotrephes — The Church Karen**. Often overlooked. Scripture says he loved to be first, talked excessively, rejected people, blocked access, and overruled authority. Karen wants to gatekeep and disguise it as leadership.

6. **Pharaoh — Ownership Over People's Movement**. "You can't leave." "You work for me." "This affects my system." Karen believes that when people exit her system, that is rebellion. Karen hates quiet departure.

7. **Laban — Familiar Control -** Laban controlled through closeness. "We're family." Karen confuses proximity with permission. Laban was shocked by disengagement. Karen often is too.

Biblical Karens have several traits in common. They are unassigned. They see clearly. They feel strongly, and they intervene wrongly. Their core belief is, *If I notice it, I own it.* Scripture disagrees.

The Christian Karen problem is that many Karens believe they are acting in righteousness. They say, "I'm standing for truth." "Someone has to say something." "Silence is agreement." But Scripture shows something else: Jesus ignored traps, withdrew often, answered briefly, and exited constantly. Paul walked away from cities, refused endless explanations, and let people misunderstand him. God Himself allows free will daily, does not escalate, does not hover.

Holiness does not require supervision; it is above the Law.

Before you speak, correct, escalate, or intervene, ask and wait for the answer to: *Am I assigned — or am I just, right?* If you're assigned there will be cost, responsibility, and accountability. If you're just right, there will be urgency, irritation, and possibly an audience, but it doesn't mean you should act. One produces fruit, the other produces exhaustion.

Anti-Karen truth is that you can be right, Christian, and discerning and still not be *involved*. Anti-Karen knows the difference. If justice requires an audience, it's probably performance.

KAREN AS A TERRITORIAL *SPIRIT*
Why Karen Thinks She Owns Everything

Karen energy is not just corrective; it is **territorial**. This is why Karen does not merely *comment;* she **claims**. She thinks she owns everything or everything that is convenient for her to own. She behaves as though spaces belong to her. She thinks conversations belong to her. She believes that processes belong to her. She thinks outcomes belong to her. She thinks that people's choices belong to her and she gets to choose for them or make decisions for others. And, of course, those decisions will benefit Karen and be convenient for Karen.

Even when none of that is true.

Let's look at the pattern of territorial *spirits* in Scripture. In the Bible, territorial *spirits* operate by asserting ownership where there is no assignment. They do not always appear violent. They appear entitled. Their language is subtle, saying or suggesting things like, *"This is how things are done here."* *"You can't just do that." "Someone needs to stop this." "This affects all of us."*

Karen doesn't ask, *Is this mine to steward?* She assumes: *This is my territory.*

Territorial *spirits* are not obsessed with people; they are obsessed with control of space. They attach to institutions, neighborhoods, churches, workplaces, and families. They are deeply attached to systems: *how we do things.*

Karen energy emerges when a person internalizes territorial authority without Divine or delegated assignment. That's why Karen often speaks as if representing "everyone." Invokes rules instead of relationships. Resents autonomy. She panics at quiet exits.

Biblical examples of territorial control (male-dominant) include: Pharaoh who didn't just rule Egypt, he claimed ownership over *movement*. He said, *"You can't leave,"* but really saying, *This labor belongs to me.*

Karen-channeling-Pharaoh reacts strongly when people disengage, as in leaving a job, leaving a church, leaving a conversation, leaving a system. To a Karen, exit feels like rebellion.

Laban controls territory through claimed familiarity, through relationship, not force.

"You are my bone and flesh." "These flocks are mine." "Your success belongs here." Karen-channeling-Laban believes proximity = permission. She believes that history = authority, or that relationship = ownership.

This is why Karen is often stunned when someone quietly leaves.

The Pharisees claimed moral jurisdiction over public life. They did not just teach the law; they policed behavior. Karen-channeling-Pharisee monitors, corrects, escalates, and performs righteousness publicly.

They believe holiness gives them territorial access to others' lives.

Karen is often unaware because *territorial spirits* rarely feel aggressive *to the host*. They feel like responsibility, concern, duty, stewardship. Karen sincerely believes she is helping, protecting, and maintaining order. Because the control is moralized, it escapes self-examination. That's why argument fails. To be from under their control, territorial *spirits* are not persuaded; they are starved by loss of access.

Jesus never negotiated territory He wasn't assigned. He crossed borders without explanation, ignored Pharisaical jurisdiction, withdrew from cities, refused public traps, and left hostile regions quietly. He did not confront every territorial claim. He simply did not recognize their authority. That is Anti-Karen behavior. Jesus is Anti-Karen energy.

Anti-Karen disarms territorial control. You do not defeat territorial *spirits* by arguing, explaining, escalating, and defending yourself. You disarm them by moving freely, exiting quietly, refusing the audience, and governing yourself. Karen loses power the moment you realize that *This was never her territory.*

Territorial Karen doesn't want control of people as much as she wants control of space. Territorial *spirits* don't ask permission. They assume ownership; and they don't want you in it for whatever reason. Karen treats public space like inherited property.

Because this is a Christian book, the uncomfortable question isn't *Have I met a Karen?* It's *Where have I claimed territory God never gave me?* That's the mirror. That's the repentance point because maybe Auntie Karen is still in there and is still redeemable. Maybe *that Karen* is you.

Karen as a *territorial spirit* explains the ownership, the escalation, the shock at exit, the exhaustion, the misery. Anti-Karen is not rebellion; it is rightly ordered authority.

KAREN IS NOT A PRINCIPALITY

Karen is <u>not</u> a principality—there is no way she has that kind of range, but she thinks she is and she thinks she has that kind of power. She is not a ruler, and least of all would she think she is a ruler of darkness. But she still feels as though she has authority in places, situations, and over people where she has no authority. Karen does not have jurisdiction.

But she is deeply confused about this. A principality, Biblically speaking, governs *territory by assignment*. Karen governs *space by assumption*.

Karen does not say, "I have authority here." She behaves as though authority is implied by presence. I saw a You Tube short where an obvious American woman was 'exercising her First Amendment Rights in what appeared to be a foreign country, over in her neighbor's yard. It did not end well for her.

A Karen believes in Manifest Destiny or possession is 9/10's of the law or something. She thinks that if she is standing there, it must be hers.

The man in the video (I don't know what country they were in) said to her, "This isn't the United States."

She thinks that if she noticed it, it must require correction. If she's uncomfortable, something must change.

That's not principality energy. That's self-appointed oversight; it is a part of the Karen Delusion. Karen's internal monologue sounds like:

- *Someone needs to address this.*
- *This shouldn't be happening.*
- *This affects everyone.*
- *I can't just let this go.*

Notice what's missing:

- assignment
- responsibility
- cost
- consequence

Principality-level authority always carries burden. Karen wants **jurisdiction without weight**. Biblical principalities do not patrol checkout lines, monitor seating arrangements, supervise tone, or correct strangers. They rule **systems**, they have a jurisdiction. They do not rule situations. Karen, by contrast, micromanages moments in regions that she has no authority to oversee. Instead, it is more like she is overseeing *vibes*.

Karen is exhausted and that might be part of her grumpiness.

Karen's favorite mistake: confusing influence with inheritance.

Principalities are established. Karen seems to roam until she, like a vigilante, with no weapon but her mouth, is irritated. Principalities are assigned. Karen is offended. Principalities govern from position. Karen governs from proximity.

This is why Karen reacts so strongly to quiet exits. When someone simply leaves, Karen experiences it as: rebellion, disrespect, loss of control. A true authority doesn't notice exits. Only insecure oversight does.

When someone believes they have authority they were never given, they will: escalate unnecessarily, moralize discomfort, confuse control with care, resist freedom in others. Karen isn't battling demons. She's battling **the terror of not being in charge.** And the tragic part? She thinks she's maintaining order, but she's actually revealing fear.

Anti-Karen clarity: Karen is not a principality. She just behaves like one, but without the credentials. Which means: You don't need to confront her. You don't need to argue theology. You don't need to submit. You simply recognize the lack of assignment.

refuse the jurisdiction. and move on. Because nothing disarms false authority faster than calm disengagement.

Karen isn't ruling in the heavenlies she's supervising the sidewalk.

HOW NOT TO *KAREN*

Even When You Are Deeply, Profoundly Tempted

Let's be honest, the temptation to *Karen* is strongest when you are technically right, the rule actually exists, someone is being sloppy, the audacity is fresh, and the trash cans are involved. This section is not about pretending you don't notice It's about **choosing not to deputize yourself**.

Step 1: Pause the Inner Monologue

If your thoughts begin with:

- "Someone needs to…"

- "This can't be allowed…"

- "I should probably say something…"

Pause.

That's not discernment; That's adrenaline.

Step 2: Ask the Assignment Question. Ask yourself—quietly, privately. **Is this my responsibility, or is it merely irritating?** If you are not funding it, fixing it, managing it, or living with the long-term consequences, …it is not your assignment.

Trash cans included.

Step 3: Imagine the Paperwork. Before acting, imagine the **entire escalation path,** emails, statements, witnesses, meetings, court dates (yes, apparently). If the punishment outweighs the offense, step away from the recycling bin.

Step 4: Choose the Exit. Anti-Karen behavior often looks like going back inside, closing the blinds, muttering "wow", and living your life. Peace is cheaper than prosecution.

Step 5: Bless and Release. If you're still bothered, try this radical technique:

"Not my circus. Not my cans."

Works every time.

KAREN SPOTTING IN THE WILD

(A Helpful Checklist)

You may be dealing with a Karen if she:

☐ Knows the rules by heart
☐ Quotes policies she didn't write
☐ Feels personally offended by disorder
☐ Uses phrases like "this affects everyone"
☐ Cannot tolerate flexibility
☐ Reacts strongly to quiet exits
☐ Treats public space like inherited property
☐ Thinks escalation is responsibility
☐ Confuses irritation with injustice
☐ Has strong feelings about trash receptacles

Bonus indicators:

Karen has clipboard energy. Possibly a tight smile--, if any. She may open graciously or like a screaming banshee out of hell. "I'm just saying..." she may mention court casually

If you checked 5 or more, you have spotted a classic Karen. Remain calm.

Here's what you should do when you spot one. *(Spoiler: Almost Nothing)*. This is the hardest lesson. Do NOT argue, explain, correct, educate, escalate, or attempt to perform logic. *Why?* Because Karen feeds on engagement, resistance, witnesses, and reaction.

Remain boring. Keep answers short. Disengage politely. Leave quietly. Live freely. Some recommended phrases you could use: "I see." "Okay." "Noted." "I'm heading out."

Attempt no interventions, clarifications, and definitely no soliloquies and no TED Talk.

The Nuclear Option (use sparingly)- If absolutely necessary, deploy, *I'm comfortable with my decision.* Then stop talking. This line ends conversations because it removes jurisdiction.

Karen-ing doesn't mean you're evil. It means you momentarily forgot your lane, your peace, your authority.

Anti-Karen isn't about being passive. It's about being so governed that you don't need to manage other people's trash.

Literally.

KAREN OF THE HALLS

Karen just walked out with a clipboard and a megaphone. It's **Karen of the Halls"**

- *"Thus arose Karen of the Halls, keeper of order, enforcer of rules, unassigned to all of it."*

- *"Karen of the Halls did not inherit the hallway. She claimed it."*

- *"Every generation produces a Karen of the Halls."*

The *hall* is for hall monitor. Did you meet this Karen in grade school? Jr. high? **Karen Hall.** Hall monitor energy before it had a lease. Karen Hall. *Hall Monitor energy never retires.*

You didn't meet Karen for the first time in adulthood. You met her in **school**. She wore a sash, carried a clipboard, or had a laminated pass. Sometimes she had nothing at all—just confidence.

Karen *Hall* did not ask to be appointed. She **volunteered herself**. **Grade School Karen *Hall.*** She reminded the teacher who was talking, who was out of their seat. who sharpened pencils too long. She loved phrases like:

- "We're not supposed to do that"

- "The rule says…"

- "I'm telling"

She wasn't mean; she was invested. Junior High Karen Hall. This is where it sharpened. She enforced dress code with enthusiasm. She noticed gum, whispers, and glances. She questioned bathroom passes. She was deputized and she felt responsible for order. She walked the halls like they were her jurisdiction. *"Where are you supposed to be?"* She didn't need to know you. She needed to correct you.

High school Karen *Hall* - she had a badge, a role, and proximity to authority, She enforced rules selectively, took notes, enjoyed reporting infractions, and confused compliance with character. This was no longer about safety. It was about control with permission.

Then she grew up. She may have been nice for a season but then Karen of the halls came out again. And now, the adult reveal. Here's the twist. Karen Hall never grew out of it. She just graduated, moved into offices, joined HOAs, sat on committees, "helped out" at church, managed Facebook groups.

Same energy; bigger *hall*.

Karen Hall is so recognizable. Because Karen Hall believes order equals morality, rules equal righteousness, supervision equals leadership. She is uncomfortable with ambiguity, freedom, and quiet exits.

Unmonitored movement alarms her spirit.

A front desk employee in a medical office did not like people in the reception area. So, she took it upon herself to solve the problem by... not scheduling people. She preferred the illusion of order over the purpose of the office, but she still collected her paycheck every week.

You cannot interview for this, because no sane person would say it out loud. Who would say that she doesn't like *people* in the reception area of a medical office. So, who would ever think to ask it?

People moving around freely, arriving, waiting, existing without her direct control feels like chaos to Reception Office Karen. It feels like exposure, vulnerability, and loss of oversight. So, she reduces the environment until it feels manageable.

No one is ever seated in a 10-chair reception area in a medical office with two doctors. She fixed it her way, even if that means eliminating the very function of the place.

Karen equates visible activity with loss of control, so she subconsciously tries to create stillness. She curates her favorite things: Silence. Emptiness. Predictability. Even when the job is literally to increase and manage flow.

Healthy people think, "My job is to manage activity." This Karen thinks, I'd feel a lot better if I prevent activity from overwhelming me."

That is a completely different operating system.

The diagnostic tell is when the environment starts becoming strangely quiet, slow, or restricted, but no one can figure out why productivity is dropping.

Because Karen is quietly reducing movement to reduce her anxiety. Just hers. It's all about her, even at work. *Karen would rather manage nothing well than manage something imperfectly or be even the slightest bit inconvenienced.*

As said, you could never ask this in an interview. Karen might not even realize that she's doing it. If she does, she's evil. I feel better when nothing is happening, as if this medical practice, which is a for-profit business is her day care and she also gets paid for being there; 30 years old.

It was later found out that Reception Office Karen was an only child and this must have been her Hundred Acre Preference. *She prefers the quiet of the Hundred Acre Wood—where nothing moves unless she moves it.*

To her, stillness feels safe. Not so much that she dislikes people, or *certain* people. It is because unpredictability feels threatening. So, she unconsciously engineers environments where nothing happens unless she permits it.

She is trying to recreate a world where everything is quiet, contained, and solitary in an office that is fast-paced, has a lot of noise, flow, interaction and sometimes unpredictability.

Karen is most at peace in environments where nothing moves without her permission.

If you're an Anti-Karen, you may have seen and recognized this. If you ever thought as a child, *"Why is she watching us?"* You already knew. Karen Hall wasn't protecting the hallway. She was **claiming it**.

Karen didn't become this way overnight. She's been monitoring halls since homeroom. Karen Hall didn't peak in high school, she just never stopped patrolling.

Yes, everyone met this Karen. Even back then, everyone knew to keep walking; keep it moving.

Karen Hall was made w*hen responsibility came too early.* Sometimes Karen Hall wasn't born a monitor, sometimes she was **parentized at home**. She's the kid who learned early that adults were distracted. Chaos was dangerous. Order kept things calm. She had 'rules' as a kid, so why don't her little sister and little brother have rules? Why are her younger siblings getting away with so much? So she made rules for them, herself.

Karen may also know that being "good" meant being useful. "Karen, her parent may have said, look out for your brother and sister, I'll be back soon." So, she stepped up. Too early.

A parentized child learns:

- *If I don't watch things, something bad will happen.*

- *If I don't speak up, no one will.*

- *Order equals safety.*

- *Responsibility equals worth.*

These kids are often praised for being mature, responsible, reliable, and "such a help." And they are. But no one teaches them when to stop, or *how* to stop.

From "helpful" to hall monitor; Karen Hall often started as the kid who reminded others of rules

- the kid who kept the peace. She took blessed are the peacemakers to a whole other level.

- the kid who told the teacher—everything. She told on everybody.

- the kid who enforced fairness

Not because she was cruel, no it was because she was anxious. Control felt like care; she was being helpful.

When the pattern hardens, here's where it goes sideways. A child who was rewarded for managing siblings, monitoring behavior, teacher's helper, and preventing, or definitely reporting trouble is the likely candidate to grow into an adult who feels responsible for everyone. She mistakes vigilance for leadership. She panics at disorder. She escalates when ignored.

For Karen of the Halls, the hallway becomes her office, her watch position. As she grows up the hall changes. Now it's the office, the restaurant, the church, the HOA, the comment section. Everywhere she goes, there she is. Same reflex--, bigger hallway.

The compassionate truth is that Karen behavior doesn't always come from entitlement. It's not really her fault either; it's learned behavior. Sometimes it comes from early pressure, unshared burden, or being loaded with emotional responsibility that didn't belong to her. That doesn't make the behavior okay, but it makes it understandable.

Understanding is not endorsement; it's context.

It's about learning to say, *"Hey, I don't have to manage this anymore."*

Yes, the condition is reversable. At some time, Karen may come to herself, wake up in her right mind and that is the moment she realizes:

- I'm no longer the hall monitor, teacher's helper, teacher's pet.

- The hallway is not mine and it is also not my problem.

- Safety doesn't require supervision; let grown people be grown.

- "Some Karens learned control before they learned rest."

- Parentized children grow up thinking peace depends on them like they are the marshal in a western or the caped crusader in a cartoon

- "Karen *Hall* was once a kid doing an adult's job."

Not every hall monitor was a tyrant. Some were just tired children who never clocked out.

Self-governance, which is a hallmark of minding your own business--, and not other people's is learned. Live and let live; God's got this.

A PRAYER FOR DELIVERANCE FROM FALSE AUTHORITY AND PARENTIZATION

Father God,
I release the weight of responsibility that was never mine to carry.
I renounce false authority, borrowed authority, and the need to manage what You did not assign.

Where I learned to control in order to feel safe,
teach me now how to rest in trust.
Where I was parentized too early,
restore to me the freedom of right-sized responsibility.

I give back every role I took on to survive.
I lay down vigilance that no longer serves me.
I choose self-governance over supervision,
peace over performance,
and clarity over control.

Teach me when to act —
and when to let go.

In the Name of Jesus, Amen.

CHILDREN OF KARENOHOLIC PARENTS

A Brief Word to the Kids Who Learned to Walk Ten Feet Behind

If you grew up with a Karen parent, you probably mastered the art of strategic distancing at a young age. Then you learned to pretend you didn't know them. Stare at your shoes. Learn to mouth "I'm so sorry" to strangers. You may have walked faster when voices got louder. Or you may have had to say, "Please don't" with your eyes.

You became fluent in a language that sounds like, *"No, Mom. It's fine." "Dad, please don't say anything." "We can just leave." If you had to do any of that, then t*his section is for you.

The silent burden for children of Karenoholic parents is that they often carry secondhand embarrassment, anticipatory anxiety, hyper-awareness of public spaces, and an instinct to de-escalate situations they didn't start. You didn't want attention—well, at least not that kind. You would have preferred invisibility to that cluster show.

You learned early that public spaces were unpredictable because your parents might suddenly decide. "We need to do something about this."

What kids learn (that they shouldn't have had to) is how to be overly polite. conflict-avoidant. apologetic for existing. hypersensitive to rules or terrified of "causing a scene". Not because they're weak, but because they were parented by escalation. You didn't learn Peace. You learned damage control.

Your parent's behavior was not your responsibility. You were not rude, ungrateful, disloyal, or unsupportive for wanting the moment to end. Wanting peace is not betrayal.

Karen Parents don't realize the cost. Karen Parents often believe they're protecting their children. they're standing up for what's right; they're modeling strength. But the child actually experiences fear of attention, social shame, and a wish to disappear. Karen Parents confuse assertiveness with safety. Children know the difference.

To the adult children reading this, remember, you are allowed to choose quiet, walk away, disengage, leave without explanation, and govern yourself differently. You do not have to repeat the pattern to be loyal. You do not have to escalate to be strong. You do not have to inherit their voice to honor their role. Breaking the cycle is not rejection. It's healing.

If you ever thought: *"Please don't embarrass me."* What you were really saying was: *"Please don't make the world unsafe." And t*hat was a reasonable request.

Some children grow up learning how to speak up. Others grow up learning how to disappear. Anti-Karen adulthood is often the moment you decide. *I no longer need to disappear.*

Some grew up thinking this is how it is, "I've got to run things, like momma." (Generational dysfunction). Karen-type behavior tends to show up where a person feels *uncertain about their authority* or *overstimulated by ambiguity*. That often happens more in public spaces than at home, but not because they're secretly different people. It's about environment + perceived control.

So, their nervous system is calmer. There's less ambiguity to react to. It's not that they're never controlling at home — it's that the triggers are lower.

In public = ambiguity + audience. Public settings introduce strangers, unclear norms, unpredictability, perceived lack of control, social visibility. For someone with a low tolerance for perceived disorder, this combination helps create that "someone needs to handle this" feeling.

Public spaces also provide witnesses, validation opportunities, and social reinforcement.

At home there's no external audience to confirm "you're right." In public, agreement or attention can quickly legitimize the impulse.

Some people do show the same behaviors at home — especially if family roles are rigid, stress is high, or control has become a general coping strategy. Others appear calm at home simply because their environment is already structured to their liking, or family members have learned to adapt around them. So, it's less "two personalities" and more two trigger levels.

The underlying mechanism is to Karens, control reduces anxiety. Predictability reduces control needs. Ambiguity increases control impulses. Home usually supplies predictability, whereas public spaces remove it.

Karen-type behavior tends to surface where people feel uncertain, overstimulated, or unassigned — which is often in public spaces.

A Prayer for the Child of a Karen

Father,

I bring You the child in me who learned too early to
manage, fix, and anticipate.
The one who believed safety depended on control,
and love depended on being in charge.

Where I learned, *"This is how it is,"*
show me now a different way.
Where I believed I had to run things to survive, teach
me how to rest without fear.

Heal the places where responsibility replaced
childhood. Release me from inherited urgency, from
generational patterns of control, from the belief that
Peace depends on my vigilance.

I am allowed to be free.
I am allowed to step back.
I am allowed to live without managing everyone else.

I choose a new pattern.
I choose wholeness over repetition.
I choose Peace over inherited pressure.

In the Name of Jesus, Amen.

Prayers for Deliverance from the Spirit of Karen

Prayer 1: **From the Need to Escalate**

Lord, deliver me from the urge to correct what I can simply leave. Remove from me the need to be heard when silence would govern better. Teach me when to speak — and when to exit without commentary. In the Name of Jesus, Amen.

Prayer 2: **From False Authority**

God, strip me of borrowed authority. I release the need to manage outcomes that are not assigned to me. Where I have confused proximity with permission, correct me. Restore to me quiet confidence and clean boundaries. In the Name of Jesus, Amen.

Prayer 3: **From Outrage Addiction**

Father, break my attachment to indignation. I renounce the thrill of being right at the cost of being free. Teach me to govern myself so I no longer seek to govern others. In the Name of Jesus, Amen.

Prayer 4: **Into Anti-Karen Freedom**

Lord, I choose self-government over public confrontation. I choose discernment over suspicion. I choose exits over escalations. I choose Peace over performance. In the Name of Jesus, Amen.

RESTAURANT KARENS

When nothing is wrong, but the cost of something must be discounted or free, enter Restaurant Karen. Restaurant Karen is a distinct subspecies. She does not arrive hungry; she arrives auditing. Her appetite is not for food; it's for leverage.

Restaurant Karen is not looking for satisfaction. She's looking for a discount with a story. If everything were perfect, she would be disappointed.

You may be dealing with a Restaurant Karen if she reads the menu like it's a legal document. Mentions how often she eats *here*. Sighs, even once, before the food arrives--, already dissatisfied. Announces disappointment early ("I *hope* this is good"). Takes one bite, pauses, then looks around. If she uses phrases like: *"This isn't what I expected, "I've never had it like this befor*e. Or she is known for saying, *Normally, it's much better.*

Brace yourself if she wants to speak to the manager before finishing the meal, especially if she still eats most of the food.

She is full, but unsatisfied. The Restaurant Karen logic loop: Order normally. Find a minor imperfection. Inflate it morally. Escalate politely. Accept comped item with dignity. Return again next week.

Karen doesn't hate the restaurant. She needs it.

Restaurant Karen exists because they believe that paying entitles them to perfection. Discomfort entitles them to compensation. Being unhappy entitles them to attention. Food becomes the battlefield because the stakes are low, authority is nearby, managers are trained to appease, consequences are minimal.

It's escalation with appetizers.

Anti-Karen energy at restaurants looks like sending food back **only if necessary.** Accepting small imperfections. Paying the bill without a performance. Tipping generously. Leaving quietly. Anti-Karen understands that n*ot every inconvenience is a negotiation.*

But Karen--, oh Karen has a whole other philosophy. Seated at the table she chose after rejecting two others like it was a game of musical chairs, she is perched on her throne. She flags the server.

"It's not bad," she says. "But it's just not," she pauses for dramatic effect--, it's just not *right*."

The server nods. "What's wrong with it?"

She gestures vaguely. "I don't know--, something." But she *will* accept a free dessert. Karen doesn't want a refund. She wants a victory. Restaurant Karen orders confidently and sends it back. If nothing is wrong, Karen will find something *adjacent*. Karen eats the meal, then reviews the experience.

A 22-year-old says, "I love writing online reviews of businesses; they make me feel powerful." Online reviews are one of the few places where a stranger has influence. Feedback is public. Businesses visibly respond. The writer feels heard, seen, and feels consequential. The *feeling* of power is real but there is an unhealthy drift to something like, "I like the feeling of affecting outcomes from a distance."

It's not about reviews. It's about discovering a channel where you can move things without relationship, responsibility, or context. *Some people don't love reviews. They love the feeling of impact without involvement.*

To be fair, everyone has had a bad meal. Everyone has sent food back. Restaurant Karen isn't about standards; she's about entitlement disguised as disappointment. Anti-Karen knows the difference and conducts herself very well.

NOT JUST CLUELESS, BUT ALSO UNAWARE

This matters — especially when it's family. Karen-behavior is often moralized control, not malicious intent. People in this pattern genuinely believe: They're helping. They're protecting. They're being responsible. They're "just saying what everyone's thinking." The control is framed as concern, it goes unexamined. That's why argument doesn't work. Awareness is not produced by confrontation — only by loss of access.

The correct response is still governance, not accusation. You do not need to convince Pharaoh. You do not need to correct Laban. You do not need to expose Karen. You simply remove access, clarify boundaries internally, and adjust your movement. When possible, leave without drama. This is exactly what Jacob did when he left Laban's ranch.

This is exactly what Moses did. This is exactly what Jesus did.

Karen's problem isn't volume. It's ownership — claimed without assignment." Or: "When someone believes they own what they were never given, control feels like virtue." That teaches without attacking.

For some people, controlling behavior can be a way to compensate for feeling small, unheard, or ineffective in other parts of life. It's not because they wake up wanting to bully, but because they don't feel influential where it really matters to them. They don't feel secure inside. They don't feel respected or steady in their own world.

So, they reach for situations where they **can** feel impactful. That can drift into harshness toward others… and often toward themselves too. The same inner voice that says, *"They're doing it wrong,"* is usually saying, *"I'm not doing enough / I'm not okay,"* on the inside.

When someone doesn't feel powerful in their own life, they may look for small places to feel powerful in other people's. Sometimes that can include being very hard on themselves without being fully aware of it.

Prayers for Deliverance (From the Ownership Spirit)

Prayer: From False Ownership Lord, deliver me from claiming what You did not assign. Remove from me the need to manage people, outcomes, or spaces that are not mine to steward. Teach me the difference between care and control. In Jesus' Name, Amen.

Prayer: From Pharaoh's Grip God, where I have resisted release, soften my hands. Where I have feared loss of control, restore trust. I renounce ownership over what belongs to You alone. In Jesus' Name, Amen.

Prayer: From Laban's Familiar Control Father, free me from entitlement born of proximity. I release the need to claim credit, access, or authority over another's life. Restore clean love and honest boundaries. In Jesus' Name, Amen.

BREAKING THE KAREN SYSTEM

Once you can see this system at work, then you can learn to govern yourself accordingly. You break it by self-government, using discernment. That is freedom.

When we look for Karens in the Bible, we don't just see female archetypes that resemble her in behavior. Karen is not best explained by female Biblical characters. Choosing only women would be inaccurate, lazy, and ironically... Pharisaical. The operating system Karen runs on is overwhelmingly **male** in Scripture because it is about institutional control, ownership, and authority without assignment. Scripture consistently critiques men with power, not women with feelings.

Karen is not "emotional." Karen is administrative.

The correct Biblical lineage (male-dominant, authority-based), as we have discussed would be Pharaoh who works by exerting ownership over people and human movement. Karen-channeling-

Pharaoh says: "You can't just leave." "You owe an explanation." "This affects me." Exit feels like insubordination. She can behave as a Laban, claiming ownership through proximity. Laban didn't dominate by force; he dominated by familiarity.

Karen-channeling-Laban says: "After all I've done…" "We're family / coworkers / community" "You can't make this decision without me." Laban was genuinely shocked when Jacob left.

Pharaoh or Laban in a Karen -- same *spirit*, different clipboard. Then there is Saul who uses insecurity + control. Saul didn't want order; he wanted control without loss of relevance. Karen-channeling Saul says: *"This shouldn't be happening." "I'm uncomfortable." "Someone needs to do something."* That "something" is usually interference.

Karen is often unaware (and genuinely miserable--, a frustrated mess. Karen is not enjoying herself. She is anxious, threatened by autonomy, distressed by ambiguity, terrified of loss of control. She is convinced that responsibility lies outside herself. She escalates because self-governance feels unsafe. That's why she behaves as if she owns everything, manages everyone, corrects constantly and is never at peace.

This is fear dressed up as authority.

Karen isn't a woman problem. She's a control problem. Karen doesn't want the manager's job. She wants the authority without the assignment. Karen escalates because she doesn't know how to govern herself. If everything feels like yours, Peace is impossible.

Karen is not a villain to defeat. Karen is a case study in what happens when authority is externalized. The antidote to this isn't confrontation; it's discernment, self-governance, clean exits, and no explanations required. It's Anti-Karen. And her tone isn't rage for rage. No, it's clarity with a raised eyebrow.

Karen is exhausted, and Anti-Karen refuses to live that way.

ESCALATION IS NOT A PERSONALITY

Some people have hobbies. Some people have talents. Karen has escalation. She doesn't start at conversation. She starts at *pressure*. She skips curiosity, context, proportion. Karen goes straight to management, policy, authority, often quickly saying, "Someone needs to know about this."

Escalation feels productive because it creates movement. Emails get sent. Voices get raised. Names get written down. But movement is not progress. Escalation is often just discomfort in a hurry.

Anti-Karen energy understands something simple and powerful: If something requires escalation, it already requires too much of me.

Healthy people ask: *Can I live with this? Can I adjust? Can I leave?*

Karen asks *Who can I involve?* Escalation is attractive when you feel invisible. You feel powerless. you feel entitled to outcomes you don't control. But escalation doesn't create authority. It borrows it.

Borrowed authority always comes with strings. Here's the quiet truth. Most situations do not improve when more people are added.

They improve when expectations are lowered. boundaries are clarified internally. Exits are taken without speeches. If you find yourself rehearsing what you'll say to management, pause and ask *Do I want resolution — or recognition?*

If it's recognition, escalation will give you a brief hit and a long hangover.

Anti-Karen people don't escalate; they reposition. Karen is more of a posture. It is the posture of externalized control and false ownership. This is borrowed authority as she tries to correct others in public.

Anti-Karen is internal governance.

Karen energy is external control, public escalation, moral performance with a *someone must fix this* attitude. Authority is borrowed from outrage.

Anti-Karen Energy requires internal governance. It demands private decision-making and clean exits. No audience is required and authority must be rooted in clarity.

Karen as a Pharisee invokes rule enforcement without assignment. Karen flowing in Pharaoh shows up as ownership over people. Karen doesn't want responsibility; she wants ownership. People who govern themselves don't need to govern others. Not necessarily by looks, Karen thinks she's Cleopatra, not for beauty, but for power, as if she even knows that Cleopatra was a pharaoh. Karen flowing in the Pharaoh pattern, which is ownership of people, claiming ownership over what God said must go free. "Who is the Lord, that I should obey Him?" Pharaoh says, *"You work for me." "You don't leave unless I allow it." "Your movement threatens my control."*

Karen, in this stream, polices people's movement. Resents autonomy. Escalates when others disengage. Feels personally offended when someone exits quietly. This is why Karen cannot tolerate someone simply leaving. Exit feels like rebellion.

Karen can also flow in the Laban pattern of ownership through proximity and familiarity. Laban never said, "I own you." He said: "You are my bone and my flesh." And then, changed wages, shifted boundaries, claimed credit for Jacob's blessing. Laban acted shocked when Jacob left, saying, *"Because we're close, I have rights." "Because I helped you once, I own outcomes." "Your success belongs partly to me."* Karen in this stream: Oversteps relational boundaries. She confuses familiarity with permission. She feels entitled to input, and is stunned when quietly disengaged. She is totally unaware that she is like this. Laban never thought he was wrong either.

JUST BECAUSE YOU'RE RIGHT DOESN'T MEAN YOU'RE INVOLVED

This is where things get tricky. Because Karen is often right. The rule *does* exist. The line *was* skipped. The policy *was* violated. The tone *was* inappropriate. Yet none of that made it her assignment. Truth is not the same thing as authority. Correctness is not the same thing as calling. And being right does not automatically enroll you in the situation.

This is where many well-meaning Christians get lost. They confuse discernment with duty, conviction with commission, seeing with being sent. The Bible is full of people who were right and still told to stand down. Many Karens sincerely believe they are being Godly. They aren't trying to be cruel. They are trying to be correct. That's why the closest Biblical mirror for Karen isn't a villain, it's the Pharisee. The Pharisees were not pagans. They were Scripture-quoting, rule-keeping, and allegedly, God-fearing people.

Jesus rebuked them more than any others because they believed that being right entitled them to intervene. They corrected publicly. They enforced rules they didn't carry. They escalated constantly. They monitored behavior instead of governing themselves. They were right about the law — and wrong about their place in it.

Karen energy says, *"Someone must address this."*

Jesus energy says, "Who sent you?" That question still matters.

There is a Christian Karen trap. When faith becomes a justification for involvement instead of a guide for restraint. Karen-Christianity sounds like "I'm just standing for truth. Someone has to say something. If I don't speak up, who will? Silence is agreement.

But Scripture says otherwise. Jesus saw plenty He didn't confront. Paul walked away from entire cities. God Himself allows free will daily without commentary. Sometimes righteousness looks like restraint.

The test of assignment is before you speak, correct, escalate, or intervene, ask one question, Am I assigned — or am I just, right? If you are assigned there will be responsibility. there will be cost. there will be accountability.

If you are merely right, there will be irritation. there will be urgency. there will be an audience. One leads to fruit. The other leads to burnout and broken relationships.

Anti-Karen energy understands that not every truth requires my participation. You can be right and still be quiet. You can see clearly and still move on. You can love God deeply and still mind your business. That's not compromise; that's Wisdom. Just because you're right doesn't mean you're involved.

Karen doesn't usually think she's wrong. Karen energy shows up most often where moral certainty outruns assignment. And Scripture is *packed* with examples of people who were technically correct… and spiritually out of line.

ONLINE EXPOSÉ KAREN

Online Exposé Karen is a real and modern species, and she deserves a very careful, very funny treatment so it doesn't turn into a how-to manual for cruelty. Online Exposé Karen does not confront privately. She documents publicly.

She believes screenshots and justice threads are truth, virality is virtue. And she is always "just informing people."

The signature moves that you may be dealing with an Online Exposé Karen if she says, *"I wasn't going to post this, but…"* Or she opens with *"People deserve to know."* There may be screenshots and conversations without consent. She uses phrases like receipts. And says things like, *This is who they REALLY are.* She frames character assassination as community service. Keeps posting *after* the point is made.

If the post outlives the offense, an Online Expose' Karen may have been involved.

Online Exposé Karen believes she is protecting others, standing for truth, holding people accountable, preventing harm. But there is no due process, no proportionality, no path to repair, no exit ramp. Just exposure.

She has a low tolerance for disorder as **she** perceives disorder. She is confusing visibility with resolution. She's mistaking attention for authority and then she turns her own discomfort into spectacle.

Karen energy with Wi-Fi is when she is *no longer asks to speak to the manager. She tags the internet.*

Public shaming feels powerful because it can create instant allies. It avoids personal risk. It removes complexity. It grants moral elevation. But it is false power because it does not create healing, correction, Wisdom, or mutual peace.

Instead, it creates fear and silence, which Karen mistakes for order.

Anti-Karen internet conduct is usually blessed and brief. Anti-Karen online behavior looks like addressing issues privately when possible, disengaging without announcement, not turning conflict into content, refusing to recruit an audience, letting some things die--, offline.

Anti-Karen understands that n*ot every wrong requires a platform.* Exposure is not the same as accountability. Karen mistakes an audience for authority. Public shaming is control with better lighting. If the goal is healing, humiliation won't get you there. Karen doesn't want resolution. She wants witnesses.

To be fair, there are real abuses, there are real harms. There are real times to warn others. Online Exposé Karen isn't about protection. It's about punishment without responsibility.

Anti-Karen knows the difference. If justice requires an audience, it's probably performance.

DARN YA

The Scene of Archived Authority

Karen is not a time traveler, but she will try to use time and chronology for her convenience. Karen quotes rules, laws, policies, and regulations from any era in human history as if they are currently in force. *Darn ya* and not the Betsy Ross mending a flag kind of darning. Karen has a key to a wardrobe (chifforobe) where she goes, not to Narnia, but to Darnya, to get rules that suit her and discomfit others. There she grabs at threads of authority and weaves her program into what she wants it to be so she can be in charge of this thing.

Whatever works for her argument becomes "the rule. You will hear things like:

- "That's against policy." *(Which policy? From when? Unknown.)*

- "You can't do that." *(Says who? Possibly 1987.)*

- "The rules say…" *(They do not. They once did. Maybe.)*

- "That's illegal." *(It is not.)*

It is as though she time-travels for authority. This is not about rules. This is about borrowing authority from the past to control the present. Karen does not reference current structure. She references whatever version of structure once gave her power. If the present rules don't support her, she goes backward in time until she finds some that do.

Here's a clue. Normal people say, "I think the policy used to be…" "Let's check what the rule is now." Karen says, "You can't do that." *(final tone, no verification, no timestamp)*. She speaks with timeless certainty about things that expired years ago—like before the Civil War, and Karen is not even civil.

To the untrained person, this sounds like experience, wisdom, knowledge, seniority, maybe even authority. But to the discerning ear, this is chronological manipulation masquerading as authority.

Karen does not follow rules. She curates them from history like a museum exhibit and brings whichever one suits her into the present. Karen is using Chronological Convenience

Karen is not a time traveler, yet she quotes rules, laws, policies, or regulations from any era, timeline, or age — as if it is current. Whatever works for her.

She curates authority like a museum exhibit.

When present reality does not cooperate with her authority, Karen does not adjust. She wants to exude authority, but she's not really under any. She wants others to obey rules, but she is not subject to them, like she's outside of time, rules and laws.

She goes to the wardrobe. She unlocks it. She rummages. She pulls out a rule from 1994--, *Oh this will work*. Or how about the office manual from a former job. The bylaws of a church she used to attend-, *Yeah, that's how we used to do it there. Let's use this.* She may locate a dusty handbook that no longer exists; it's not even in print anymore. *Ah hah!* Then she remembers something her grandmother once said, or something she once heard in passing.

She brings it back from Darnya like it is freshly printed legal code. Sadly, the goal of what she has collected is to *Darnya*, darn anyone who is doing anything she doesn't like.

Karen does not live in current structure. She lives in archived authority. The wardrobe is where she stores expired policies that she still finds useful. There are outdated expectations, but someone should fulfill them, yes? She has stacks of old hierarchies, former privileges, and irrelevant standards. All of these things make her feel sturdy. She likes them. She's saved them in Darnya--, all for future use.

She uses them, *at will,* as weapons in the present.

You may spend hours confused because "That's not how things work anymore..." You're correct, but Karen is not operating in *anymore*. She is operating in Darnya.

As an Anti-Karen you will notice this and say, "That's not the rule now."

Then Karen responds sharply with, "Well, it used to be." As if that ends the discussion, when that wasn't even a discussion. Karen doesn't adjust to the present. She visits Darnya and brings back whatever rule will make today uncomfortable for everyone else.

Karen believes she is a master of Archived Authority. *Her manual: How to Be in Power —* Always, like she's a quantum leaper, jumping eras, even if she's in <u>error</u>.

Karen keeps a private archive of old policies, former expectations, things that *used to* be true, things that were *once* enforced, and things that *sound* official. Like whatever she finds in her wardrobe on the way to Darnya--, clean, pressed, but years out of fashion. When she needs authority, she doesn't check what's current. She checks what's useful.

The rules Karen retrieves aren't sloppy. They aren't chaotic. They're immaculately maintained. That's what makes them so convincing. They look official, they look respectable, they even look "proper." They just don't belong to this time. They're simply expired.

As an Anti-Karen you can tell Darnya Karen that 1850 called—no they didn't call, they *wrote*—a letter in longhand and sent it pony-express and asked for their archaic rules back.

With archived authority, she is not trying to be correct. She is trying to remain in control. If present-day reality removes her leverage, she time-jumps. Not to learn, but to retrieve.

She used to be in charge. The role changed. The structure changed. The authority moved on. She received the memo. She just never read it. So, she continues to operate from a position that no longer exists, enforcing rules from a seat she no longer occupies.

As an Anti-Karen, you will feel confused because you're trying to respond to today while Karen is arguing from yesterday, yesteryear, ten years ago, a former workplace, an old church culture, and a family rule from childhood. Amazing how well she presents it with present-tense certainty.

In your Anti-Karen authority you say, "I beg your pardon; that's not how it works now."

Karen says, "Well, it should." "That's how it's always been done."

Karen maintains power by maintaining access to expired authority.

She will jump eras, even if she is in error.

CROOKED LINES

A man tells his newlywed wife, I'm going to be checking the linen closet from time to time to see if you are folding the towels and the sheets correctly. In this pattern, the towels are not towels. They become a measure of control, a measure of order, a measure of safety, a measure of whether the world is "right. "

So, when one towel isn't "right," the conclusion is not, Let me refold this. The conclusion is everything is wrong. The closet, the house, the marriage--, everything.

It's about linking minor imperfection to major instability.

A grounded person can say, "That's folded differently than I like. Or, the linen closet could look a lot neater than it does. But the catastrophic generalizer feels the towels are off, the blue ones are not separated from the white ones --, everything is off.

When small imperfections feel like large threats, control becomes the substitute for safety.

A Karen, male or female may sense or deem that something is fundamentally wrong, then they project that onto everything: now everything is wrong.

It's like a five-year-old kid who draws a line on a piece of paper then says, *"I didn't mean to do that, or that's the wrong color."* So, he tears the sheet out of the drawing book and throws it away, saying, *"I must start over."*

A normal person sees one crooked line or one line that is blue when the child wanted it to be green. A normal person or an Anti-Karen might see one small imperfection. A Karen will have an outsized reaction and will throw the baby and the bathwater out; the entire effort is discarded. The mistake doesn't feel small to Karen. Actually, when Karen is assessing situations there may not be a mistake or a distortion or a problem at all, but that is not what Miss Karen sees. If any one thing is not how she wants it, that is proof that the entire thing is ruined.

So instead of correcting the line, the page is sacrificed. That's a child. Karen is not a child.

In adult Karens, this shows up as abandoning projects over minor flaws, declaring systems broken over small issues, treating relationships as failed over fixable things. The internal rule for that type of person is, *If it's not right, it's worthless.*

Karen would rather destroy the page than tolerate a crooked line.

"Why is she so intense about small things?" Because to her, small things are the last place she can still feel in control. She is in survival mode, in her mind. There is no real threat, but if this one thing goes wrong, everything can or will or probably will go wrong. This is fear wearing the costume of authority.

BORROWED SAFETY

Karen says:

- "I can't focus with *that* going on."

- "This whole place is a mess."

- "Nothing works right around here."

- "How can anyone think like this?"

But the "mess" is out of sight because it is completely in another room. It could be in another department. The turmoil is in another person's life. It is in an area she is not responsible for.

Karen does not separate zones of responsibility; it is as though she cannot separate them. If anything, anywhere feels out of order, she feels out of safety. So, she tries to correct things that are not hers, are not related, are not her assignment, are not affecting her function.

This is fear looking for relief through control.

Healthy people can say, "That's over there. I'm over here."

Karen cannot. Controlling-Karen cannot. To her, everything feels connected because internally, everything feels unstable.

Anti-Karens have a stronger focus, and they can mind their own business without worrying about other people's. A regular *Karen confuses proximity with responsibility.*

At home, a grounded person can say, "The garage is cluttered, I'll have to get those Amazon boxes out of it this weekend." They realize that the garage is not affecting their home office on the other side of the house. They may say, "I'm still able to work in my home office (which is neat and clean and not in the garage."

Karen says, "The garage is cluttered. Therefore, nothing in this house works." That is textbook Karen.

For Karen, it's sadly almost like: "When I was a little girl (and felt safe), this never happened. Things were never like this, but now that 'daddy' is not here to protect me, (and my husband (if she had one, won't), guess I gotta do it myself."

Fear is a strong emotion for any of us, but especially for Karen because she's lost her rails. Actually, she doesn't think she needs any, she thinks no rails means she's finally free as she runs toward the situation at hand, she sees her braces breaking away like Forrest Gump. But those are not restraining braces, those are guardrails of civility, common sense, and human decency that she is casting off.

Her emotional root behind this perceived or acquired Archived Authority is fear.

As far as borrowed safety goes, Karen is trying to *make it like it was*. She's trying to recreate a time when someone else was in charge. When she felt safe, when someone else enforced order; but those people are gone. So, she tries to become *them* -- not with Wisdom—no, Wisdom is a guardrail. Karen is trying to become safety using **rules** applied to other people. Karen thinks like this: *If the people around me would behave a certain way, then I will be okay and my environment will be okay. And safe.*

Karen cannot function over here because of what is happening over there — even when the two have nothing to do with each other. She is suffering from environmental displacement.

What is happening is not about policy, it's about replacing lost protection with artificial control.

Karen cannot recreate the father, the husband, the authority figure that made her feel safe. She cannot recreate the structured environment from yesteryear. So, she recreates the *feeling* of safety by enforcing structure on everyone around her.

The emotional tone is out of proportion to the situation. She is not responding to what's happening.

She is responding to what used to keep her safe. And to what she fears will cascade if someone doesn't solve this *'problem'* (which is a non-problem) right now.

Karen is not trying to control you. She is trying to recover a sense of feeling safe that she lost years ago.

Karen is so afraid; she is fear in a blazer, with or without the clipboard and the bullhorn.

We may see correction, intensity, rule-quoting, and she wants us to see authority, although she has no jurisdiction—she has crossed the county lines and in her blind rage, she didn't see the signs.

But you did. As an Anti-Karen, you are like: *Who is this woman*? You see her hovering and you reject her unsolicited management.

What's there is fear; managed fear. It's the kind of fear that learned long ago: *If I keep everything in order, nothing bad can happen.*

She clings to rules because rules feel like railings on a staircase. Without them, she feels like she might fall. So, she installs rules-railings, Karen-railings like plastic baby gates everywhere, on everyone.

The truth is that the situation is small, but her response is survival-sized, not just upset-sized but upsized as well.

You're talking about a preference.

You're across the park with your family, flipping burgers.

She's responding like it's a threat--, running towards you and your family. **She** is the threat while accusing you of being the threat.

Call her what you want, and I'm sure Karen has been called a lot of things--, a lot of names. But know this: she probably was or maybe still is someone's sweet Auntie. Maybe the sweet one is still in there and can be redeemed. We certainly have all needed redemption's Grace.

Still, the street, the park, the settings she chooses are no place to get redemption; she needs Jesus. We all do.

Karen's authority is a coping mechanism for fear she never learned to name. She is wrong as hell and she's afraid.

Karen is so afraid.

DO NOT LEAVE IF YOU SHOULD STAY-
DO NOT STAY IF YOU SHOULD LEAVE

Most people think leaving is easy, but it's not. Leaving loudly is easy. Leaving with a speech, an email, a post, a debrief, a prayer request, and a witness list? Very easy. Leaving quietly requires something rarer: self-governance.

Quiet exits give you something better: freedom without negotiation. Karen hates quiet exits because they deny jurisdiction.

Leaving quietly feels so uncomfortable (at first) because Karen culture teaches: that you must explain yourself. You must justify your choice and soften the blow. You must manage other people's feelings. Explanation is not required when authority is absent. Leaving quietly deprives others of control. It refuses the performance. It denies escalation and withholds the audience

If you can leave quietly, it proves that you were never trapped.

Leaving quietly is an internal decision, external simplicity. It is clarity without commentary. It is movement without messaging. It is not simply ghosting with malice, punishment, manipulation, or passive aggression. It's simply choosing not to invest further.

You don't owe a manifesto, a final conversation, a list of grievances or a teaching moment. Especially to people who were never assigned authority over you.

The following is the Biblical patterns on leaving without announcement. Scripture is full of quiet exits. Jesus slipped away from crowds, passed through hostile regions, refused traps, and left cities without explanation.

Paul shook the dust and moved on. He did not argue endlessly, or wait for consensus

Jacob left Laban while he was distracted. He didn't debate, didn't announce or justify.

Quiet exits are Biblical, not cowardly. And, they preserve life.

Karen, on the other hand, panics when you leave quietly. Because quiet exits say something devastating to her, even without words: *You, Ms. Karen, were never in charge.* Karen escalates when explanations are withheld, compliance is refused, authority is not acknowledged. Silence feels like disrespect only to those who expected control.

Anti-Karen people understand this: You don't owe explanations to unassigned authority. When you stop managing the story, you start managing your life.

The Anti-Karen exit script. If words are absolutely required, keep them boring. Use one of these: *This no longer works for me. I'm moving in a different direction. I've made my decision. I won't be continuing.* Give no reasons, no footnotes, and no defense. Boredom is a boundary.

Karen escalates to stay relevant. Anti-Karen exits to stay free. One seeks control. The other chooses Peace. And here's the quiet flex: The calmer your exit, the less authority they ever had.

THE ANTI-KAREN RECOVERY PLAN

(One page. Tape it to the fridge if needed.)

1. Notice the urge to intervene

2. Ask: *Is this my business?*

3. If unsure, assume **no**

4. Choose silence or distance

5. Enjoy your Peace

6. Repeat as necessary

The good news?
This is recoverable.

Recovery looks like:

- noticing the urge

- pausing

- not speaking

- choosing distance

- going home

No announcement required.

BENEDICTION: THE PEACE OF MINDING YOUR BUSINESS

May you be delivered
from the need to correct
what you were never assigned to steward.

May you be freed
from borrowed authority,
false urgency,
and the exhaustion of managing what is not yours.

May your discernment grow quieter,
your exits cleaner,
and your Peace less dependent on agreement.

May you learn to notice
without intervening,
to see clearly
without needing to be involved.

May you leave without speeches,
choose without permission,
and move without explanation.

May you govern yourself so well
that you no longer feel tempted
to govern others.

And when you are tempted to escalate,
may you remember:

You don't need to speak to the manager.
You manage yourself.

Go in Peace.

In the Name of Jesus, **Amen**.

Dear Reader

Thank you for acquiring and reading this book, I pray it has blessed you to follow the possible path of what happened to sweet Auntie Karen and how she turned into the notorious *Karen*. I pray that you, yourself are Anti-Karen and you behave yourself well wherever life leads you.

May God bless you, richly.

Shalom,

Dr. Marlene Miles

Prayerbooks by this author

There are some books that are only prayers. You just open up the book and pray.

Prayer Manuals

FAKE FRIENDS: *Prayers Against Betrayers*

HOLIDAY WARFARE Prayer Manual (humorous) Surviving Family Gatherings All Year Long (without catching a case)

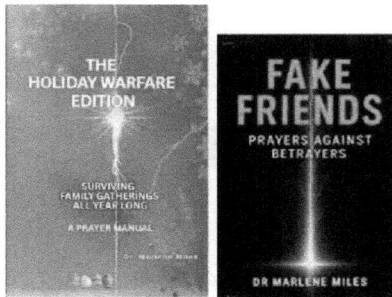

SOUL TIE Prayer Manual (The) Part of a 3-part series including a workbook.

MAD at DADDY Prayer Manual – part of a 3-part series including a workbook.

Healing the Sibling & Relative Wound Prayer Manual

Healing the Father-Son Wound Prayer Manual

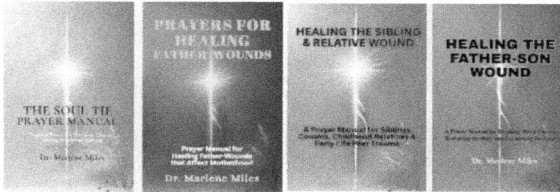

Prayers Against Barrenness: *For Success in Business and Life*

Breaking Curses of the Mother Prayer Manual

Prayers Against Barrenness: For Success in Business and Life

Fruit of the Womb: Prayers Against Barrenness

Beauty Curses, *Warfare Prayers Against*
https://a.co/d/5Xlc2OM

Courts of Marriage: Prayers for Marriage in the Courts of Heaven *(prayerbook)* https://a.co/d/cNAdgAq

Courtroom Warfare @ Midnight *(prayerbook)* https://a.co/d/5fc7Qdp

Demonic Cobwebs *(prayerbook)* https://a.co/d/fp9Oa2H

Every Evil Bird https://a.co/d/hF1kh1O

Gates of Thanksgiving

Spirits of Death, Hell & the Grave, Pass Over Me and My House

Throne of Grace: Courtroom Prayer

Warfare Prayer Against Poverty
https://a.co/d/bZ61lYu

Other books by this author

Abundance of Jesus (The)
https://a.co/d/5gHJVed

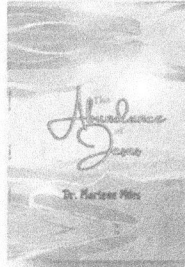

AK: The Adventures of the Agape Kid

Already Married in the Spirit: *Why You May Not Be Married in the Natural*

AMONG SOME THIEVES https://a.co/d/dkYT4ZV

Ancestral Powers

Anti-Marriage, *The Spirit of*

Backstabbers https://a.co/d/gi8iBxf

Barrenness, *Prayers Against*
https://a.co/d/feUltIs

Battlefield of Marriage, *The*

Beware of the Dog: Prayers Against Dogs in the Dream.

Bless Your Food: *Let the Dining Table be Undefiled*
https://a.co/d/6oPMRDv

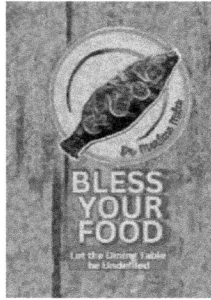

Blindsided: *Has the Old Man Bewitched You?*
https://a.co/d/5O2fLLR

Break Free from Collective Captivity

Broken Spirits & Dry Bones

By Means of a Whorish Father

Caged Life: Get Out Alive!
https://a.co/d/bwPbksX

Casting Down Imaginations

Christ of God (*The*) 3-book series

Christ of God, (*The*) Box Set, includes all three books

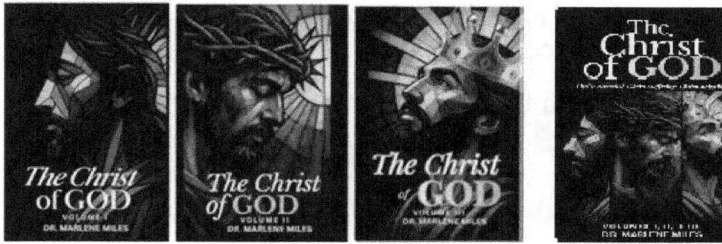

Churchzilla, The Wanna-Be, Supposed-to-be
Bride of Christ https://a.co/d/eAf5j3x

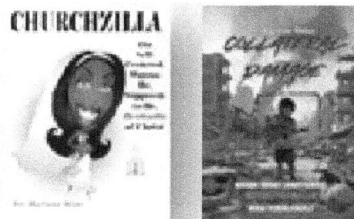

Collateral Damage: *When What Happened Spiritually Was Your Fault*

Demonic Cobwebs (prayerbook)

Demonic Time Bombs

Demons Hate Questions

Devil Loves Trauma, *The*

Devil Weapons: Unforgiveness, Bitterness,...

The Devourers: Thieves of Darkness 2

Do Not Swear by the Moon

Don't Refuse Me, Lord (4 book series)

https://a.co/d/idP34LG

Dream Defilement

The Emptiers: *Thieves of Darkness, 1*
https://a.co/d/5I4n5mc

Entanglements: *Illegal Knots Limiting Your Life*

Evil Touch

Failed Assignment

Fantasy Spirit Spouse https://a.co/d/hW7oYbX

FAT Demons (The): *Breaking Demonic Curses*
https://a.co/d/4kP8wV1

The Fold (5-book series)

- The Fold (Book 1)
- Name Your Seed (Book 2)
- The Poor Attitudes of Money (3)
- Do Not Orphan Your Seed (4)
- For the Sake of the Gospel (5)
- My Sowing Journal

Gang Ups: Touch Not God's Anointed

Gathered: No Longer Scattered
https://a.co/d/1i5DPIX

Getting Rid of Evil Spiritual Food

https://a.co/d/i2L3WYQ

got HEALING? Verses for Life

got LOVE? Verses for Life
https://a.co/d/8seXHPd

got HOPE? Verses for Life

got money? https://a.co/d/g2av41N

Has   My   Soul   Been   Sold?
https://a.co/d/dyB8hhA

Here Come the Horns: *Skilled to Destroy*
https://a.co/d/cZiNnkP

Hidden Sins: Hidden Iniquity

https://a.co/d/4Mth0wa

How to Dental Assist

How to Dental Assist2: Be Productive, Not Wasteful

How To Stay Prayed Up

How to STOP Being a Blind Witch or Warlock

I Take It Back

In Multiplying I Will Multiply Thee

Irresistible: Jesus' Triumphal Entry
https://a.co/d/dO9IfEC

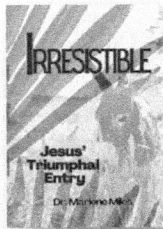

KNOW YOUR BATTLE: Stop Swinging Blindly —
and Win Against Opponents, Adversaries &
Enemies (Workbook) https://a.co/d/eOwFKlV

Legacy

Let Me Have A Dollar's Worth
https://a.co/d/h8F8XgE

Level the Playing Field

Living for the NOW of God
https://a.co/d/6bK5duE

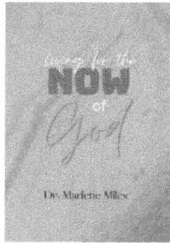

Lose My Location https://a.co/d/crD6mV9

Love Breaks Your Heart

Mad At Daddy: Healing Father-Wounds that Affect Motherhood (book, workbook & prayer manual)

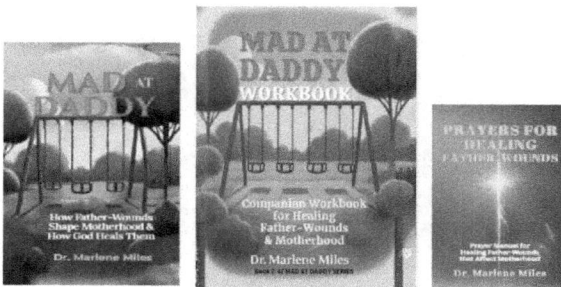

Made Perfect In Love

Mammon https://a.co/d/29yhMG7

Man Safari, *The*

Marriage Ed.: *Rules of Engagement & Marriage*

Made Perfect in Love

Money Hunters: Beware of Those

Money on the Altar https://a.co/d/4EqJ2Nr

Mulberry Tree, *The* https://a.co/d/9nR9rRb

Motherboard (The) - *Soul Prosperity Series*

Name Your Seed

Occupy: *Until I Return* https://a.co/d/bZ7ztUy

One Defining Day: *A Day When Dreams Come True*

Opponent, Adversary, or Enemy?: Fight The Right Battle with the Right Weapons

https://a.co/d/byQqEE2 & companion workbook: Know Your Battle

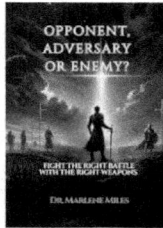

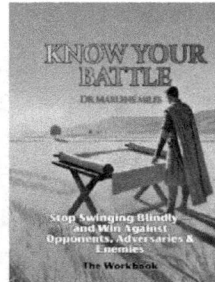

Plantation Souls

Players Gonna Play

Portals: Shut the Front Door: Prayers to Close Evil Portals.

Power Money: Nine Times the Tithe

https://a.co/d/gRt41gy

The Power to Get Wealth
https://a.co/d/e4ub4Ov

Powers Above

The Robe, Part 1, The Lessons of Joseph

The Robe, Part II, The Lessons of Joseph

Seasons of Grief

Seasons of Siege: God Is Coming

Seasons of Waiting

Seasons of War

Second Marriage, Third--, *Any Marriage*
https://a.co/d/6m6GN4N

Seducing Spirits: Idolatry & Whoredoms
https://a.co/d/4Jq4WEs

Shut the Front Door: *Prayers to Close Portals*
https://a.co/d/cH4TWJj

Sift You Like Wheat

Six Men Short: What Has Happened to all the Men?

SLAVE

Sleep Afflictions & Really Bad Dreams
https://a.co/d/f8sDmgv

Soul Prosperity soul prosperity series 3

https://a.co/d/5p8YvCN

Soul Ties: How Soul Ties Form, and How To Break Them (book, workbook & prayer manual)

Souls In Captivity

The Spirit of Anti-Marriage

The Spirit of Poverty https://a.co/d/abV2o2e

Spiritual Thieves https://a.co/d/eqPPz33

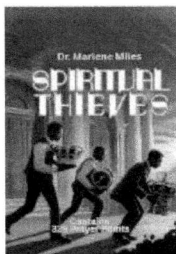

StarStruck- Triangular Power series.

SUNBLOCK- Triangular Power series.

The Swallowers: *Thieves of Darkness,* 3

Take It Back

This Is NOT That: How to Keep Demons from Coming at You

Time Is of the Essence

Too Many Wives: *Why You Have Lady Problems*

Tormenting Spirits   https://a.co/d/dAogEJf

Toxic Souls

Triangular Power *(series),* Powers Above, SUNBLOCK, Do Not Swear by the Moon, STARSTRUCK

TRIBE: *What Covenants Are Governing You...?*

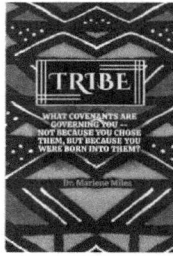

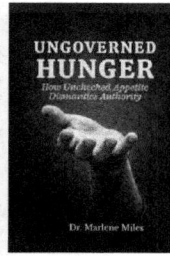

Unbreak My Heart: *Don't Let Me Die*

Uncontested Doom

Ungoverned Hunger: *How Appetite Dismantles Authority*

Unguarded Hours, *The*

Unseen Life, *The* (forthcoming)

Upgrade: How to Get Out of Survival Mode Toxic Souls (Book 2 of series) , Legacy (Book 3 of series)

The Wasters: *Thieves of Darkness,* Bk 2
https://a.co/d/bUvI9Jo

What Have You to Declare? What Do You Have With You from Where You've Been?

When I Was A Child, *I Prayed As a Child*

When the Devourer is Rebuked

https://a.co/d/1HVv8oq

WTH? Get Me Out of This Hell
https://a.co/d/a7WBGJh

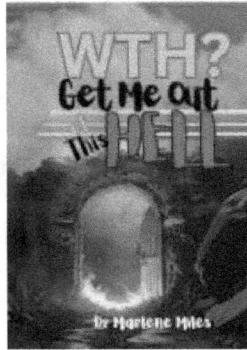

The Wilderness Romance *(series)* This series is about conducting a Godly relationship and marriage with someone who is a Wilderness person. It is about how to recognize it and navigate through it. These books are about how not to get caught up in such.

- *The Social Wilderness*
- *The Sexual Wilderness*
- *The Spiritual Wilderness*

Other Series

The Fold (a series on Godly finances)
https://a.co/d/4hz3unj

Soul Prosperity Series https://a.co/d/bz2M42q

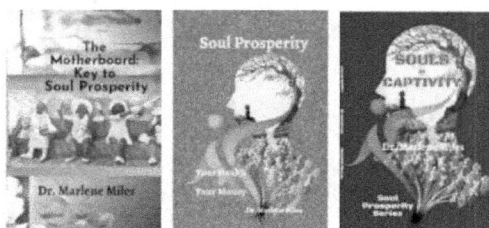

Spirit Spouse books

https://a.co/d/9VehDSo

https://a.co/d/97sKOwm

Battlefield of Marriage, The

https://a.co/d/eUDzizO

Players Gonna Play

https://a.co/d/2hzGw3N

Sent Spirit Spouse (can someone send you a spirit spouse? This book is not yet released.)

Matters of the Heart, Made Perfect in Love
https://a.co/d/70MQW3O , Love Breaks Your Heart https://a.co/d/4KvuQLZ, Unbreak My Heart https://a.co/d/84ceZ6M Broken Spirits & Dry Bones https://a.co/d/e6iedNP

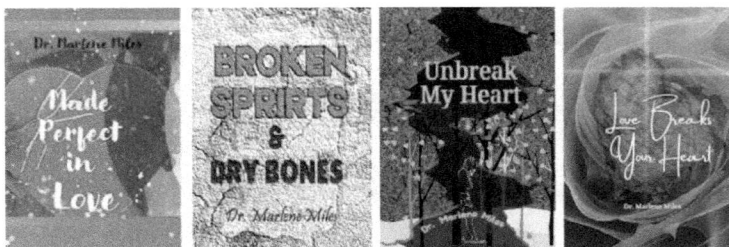

Thieves of Darkness series

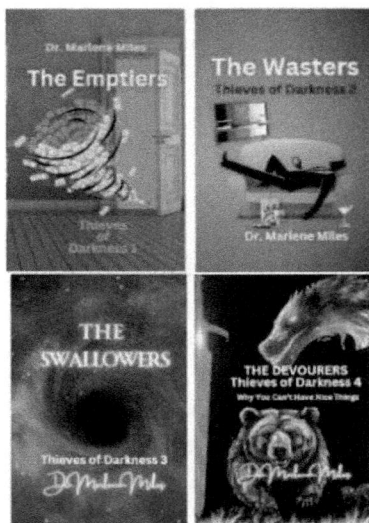

The Emptiers https://a.co/d/heio0dO

The Wasters https://a.co/d/5TG1iNQ

The Swallowers https://a.co/d/1jWhM6G

The Devourers: Why We Can't Have Nice Things
https://a.co/d/87Tejbf

Spiritual Thieves

Red Flags: The Track Is Not Safe (book & workbook)

Triangular Powers https://a.co/d/aUCjAWC

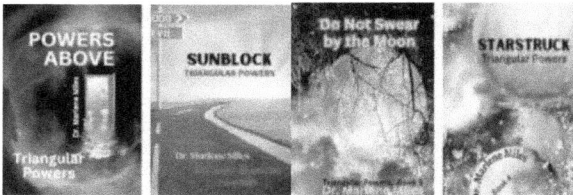

Upgrade (series) *How to Get Out of Survival Mode*
https://a.co/d/aTERhXO

We Get Along, Right? Compatibility for Couples –
(book & workbook)

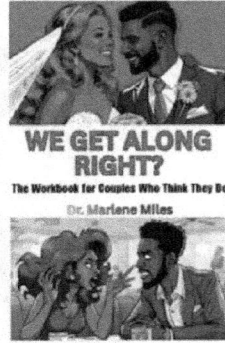

Dr. Marlene Miles is a teacher, author, and spiritual thinker known for her grounded, discerning approach to prayer and spiritual formation. Her work emphasizes clarity, restraint, and maturity in faith—helping believers move beyond emotionalism and performance into a steady, practiced walk with God.

With a deep respect for Scripture and a practical understanding of daily life, Dr. Miles writes for those who want their prayer life to be formed, not dramatized. Her teaching encourages spiritual maintenance, discernment, and responsibility—so faith remains strong not only in crisis, but in everyday living.

www.ingramcontent.com/pod-product-compliance
Lightning Source LLC
LaVergne TN
LVHW052028080426
835513LV00018B/2223